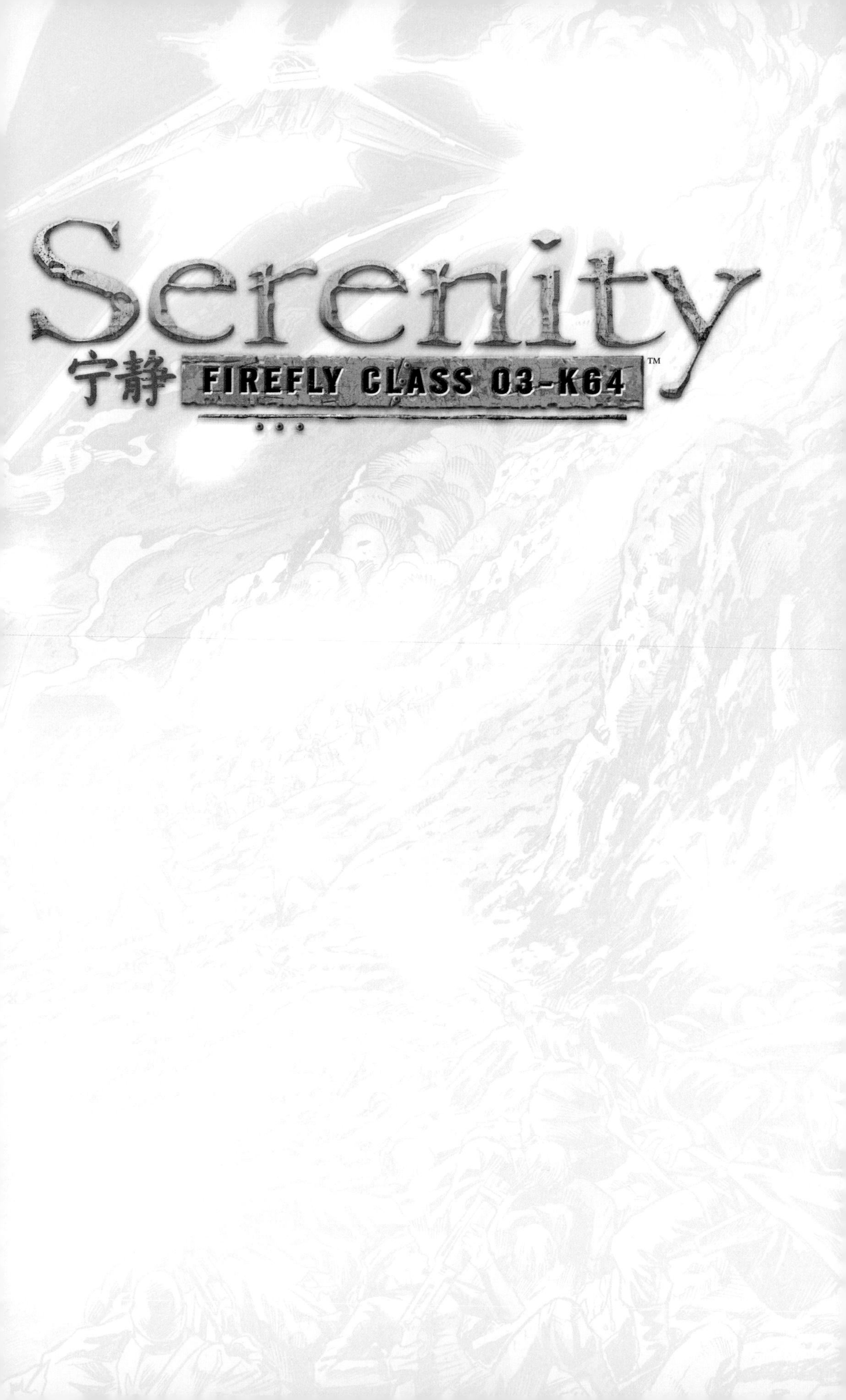

Serenity

宁静 FIREFLY CLASS 03-K64™

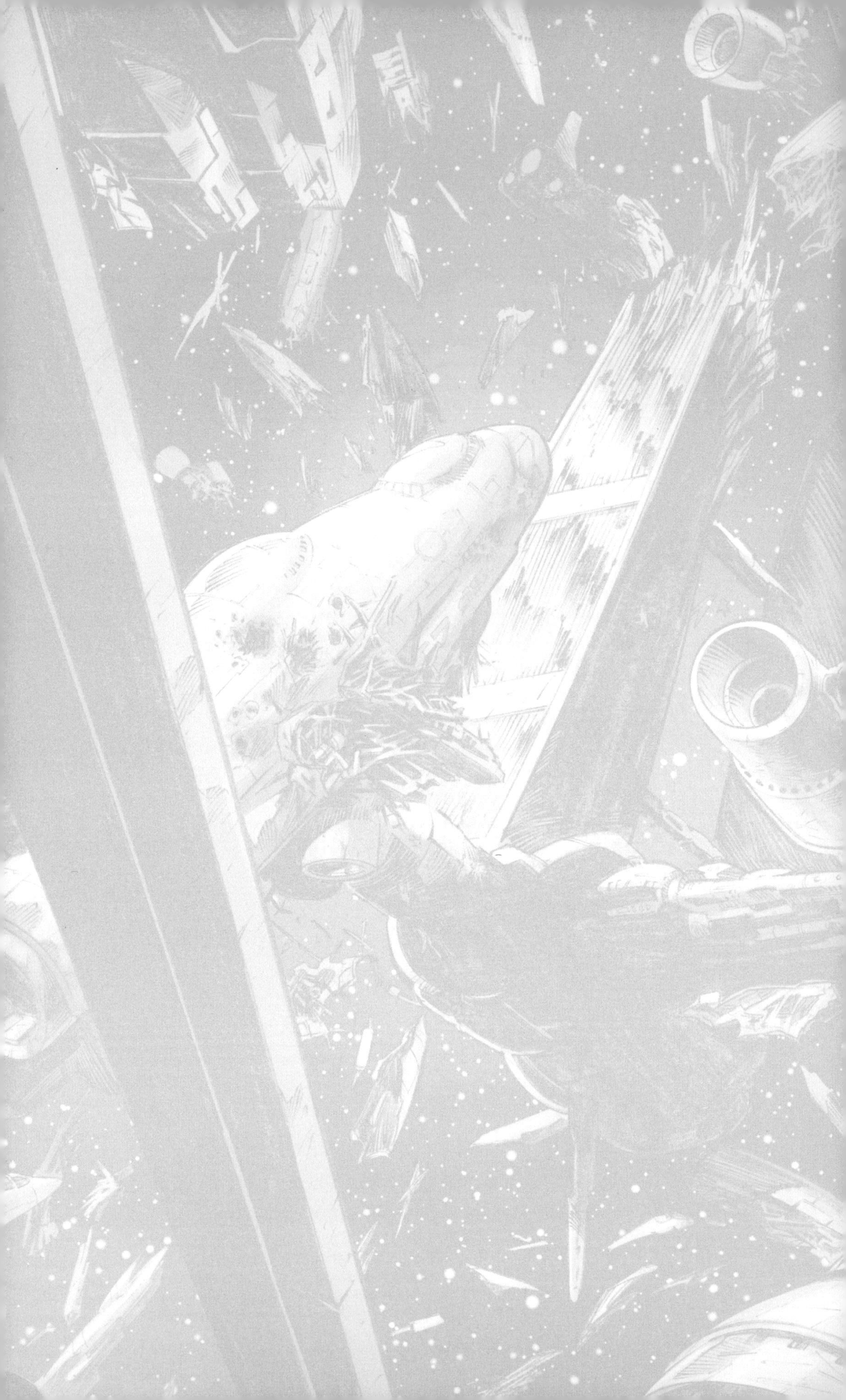

Serenity

宁静 FIREFLY CLASS 03-K64 ™

THOSE LEFT BEHIND

STORY
JOSS WHEDON & BRETT MATTHEWS

SCRIPT
BRETT MATTHEWS

ART
WILL CONRAD

COLORS
LAURA MARTIN

LETTERS
MICHAEL HEISLER

COVER ART
ADAM HUGHES

DARK HORSE BOOKS

PRESIDENT & PUBLISHER
MIKE RICHARDSON

EDITORS
SCOTT ALLIE & SIERRA HAHN

ASSISTANT EDITOR
FREDDYE LINS

COLLECTION DESIGNER
JUSTIN COUCH

SPECIAL THANKS TO CINDY CHANG AT UNIVERSAL STUDIOS
AND MATT DRYER AND DAVE MARSHALL AT DARK HORSE COMICS.

———————

NEIL HANKERSON Executive Vice President • TOM WEDDLE Chief Financial Officer • RANDY STRADLEY Vice President of Publishing • MICHAEL MARTENS Vice President of Book Trade Sales • ANITA NELSON Vice President of Business Affairs • DAVID SCROGGY Vice President of Product Development • DALE LAFOUNTAIN Vice President of Information Technology • DARLENE VOGEL Senior Director of Print, Design, and Production • KEN LIZZI General Counsel • MATT PARKINSON Senior Director of Marketing • DAVEY ESTRADA Editorial Director • SCOTT ALLIE Senior Managing Editor • CHRIS WARNER Senior Books Editor • DIANA SCHUTZ Executive Editor • CARY GRAZZINI Director of Print and Development • LIA RIBACCHI Art Director • CARA NIECE Director of Scheduling

Serenity: Firefly Class 03-K64 Volume 1—Those Left Behind

Serenity © 2005–2007 Universal Studios. Firefly and Serenity: Firefly Class 03-K64 are trademarks of Twentieth Century Fox Film Corporation. Dark Horse Books® and the Dark Horse logo are registered trademarks of Dark Horse Comics, Inc. All rights reserved. No portion of this publication may be reproduced or transmitted, in any form or by any means, without the express written permission of Dark Horse Comics, Inc. Names, characters, places, and incidents featured in this publication either are the product of the author's imagination or are used fictitiously. Any resemblance to actual persons (living or dead), events, institutions, or locales, without satiric intent, is coincidental.

Published by Dark Horse Books
A division of Dark Horse Comics, Inc.
10956 SE Main Street
Milwaukie, OR 97222

DarkHorse.com

To find a comics shop in your area, call the
Comic Shop Locator Service toll-free at (888) 266-4226.

First hardcover edition: November 2007
Second hardcover edition: August 2012

ISBN 978-1-59582-914-6

1 3 5 7 9 10 8 6 4 2
Printed in the USA

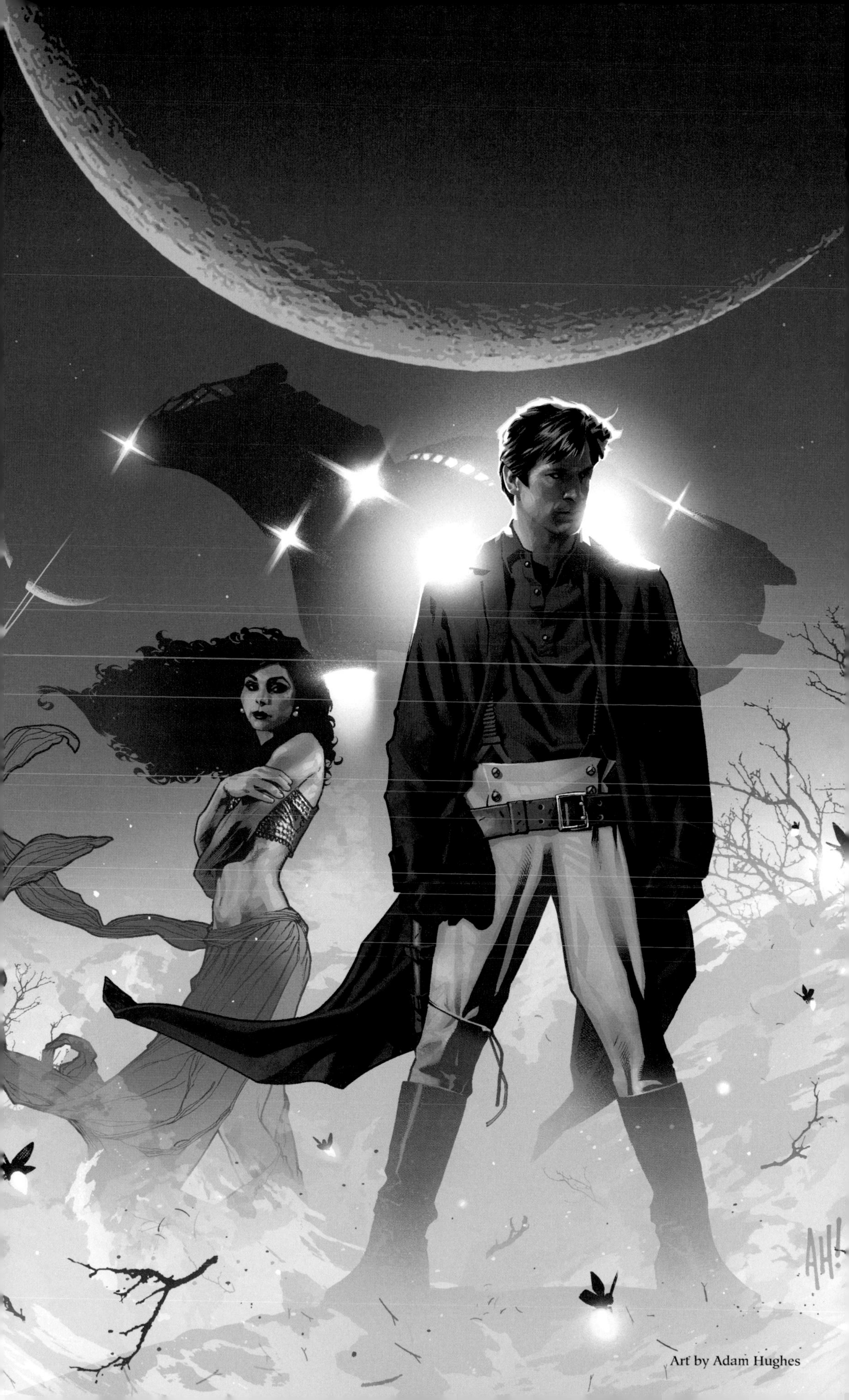

Art by Adam Hughes

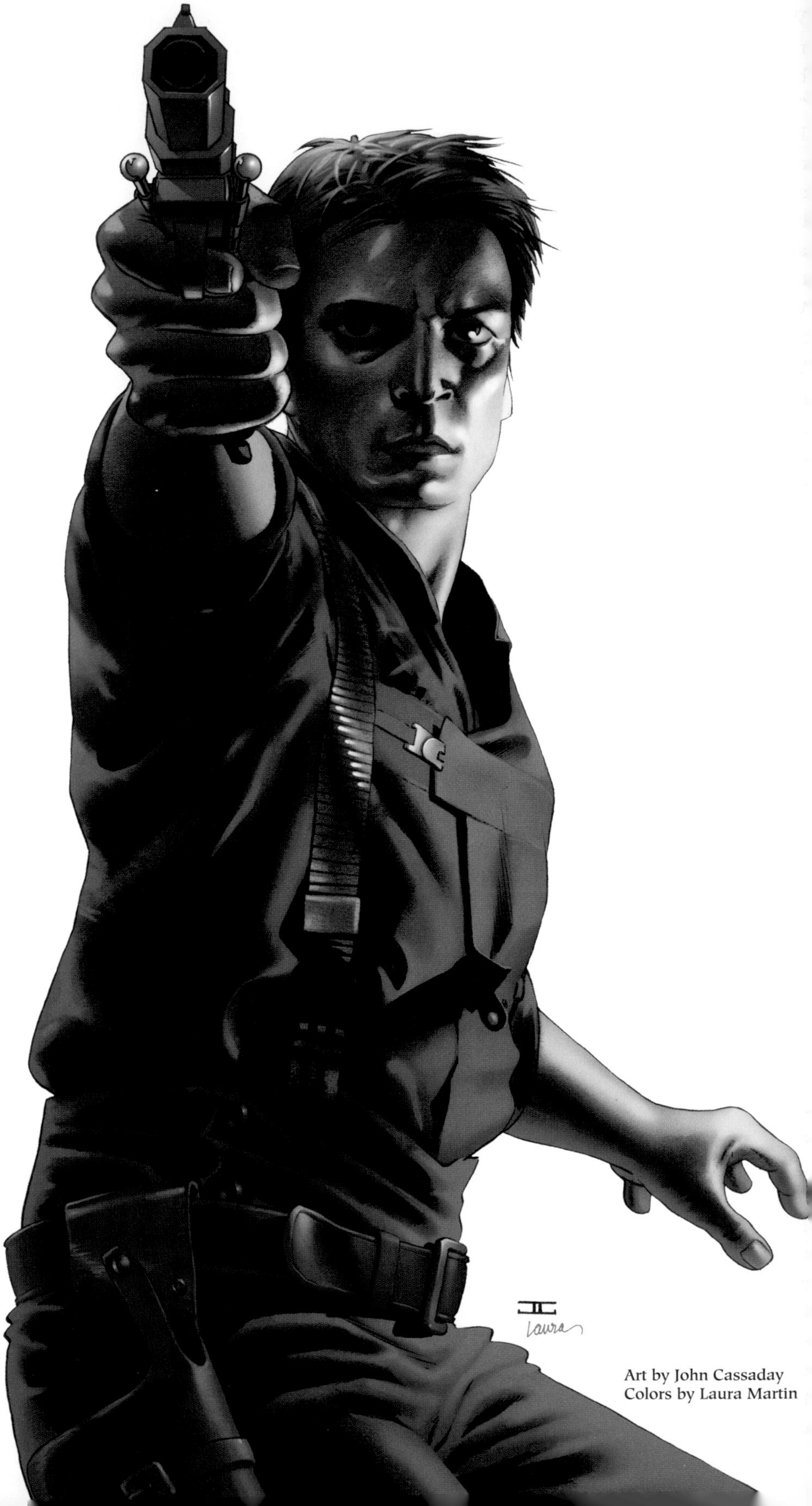

Art by John Cassaday
Colors by Laura Martin

INTRODUCTION

When I was very young, before I could read, I remember being interested in comic books. Our bedtime was not negotiable, but we could delay "lights out" for another half hour if we read anything. I mostly looked at the pictures; I could make out "a" and "the," and then simply tried to piece together a story. I could tell that Jughead liked to eat, Archie was broke, Betty was nice, and Veronica was mean. There are only so many times you can read the same ones, though, so my dad would take my brother and me to Whyte Avenue. Not too far down from Uncle Albert's Pancake House (burned down since then) was the Wee Book Inn, a store that had an odor a bit like someone's grandmother's house. Not mine, but someone's. I remember the dirty orange carpet, frayed and ragged. The wooden shelves were tall and packed with worn covers of books read many times over. Pages were yellowed and paperbacks had arched spines like old swaybacked horses. It was an old-folks' home for secondhand books, with that smell of old newsprint and slightly musty wood. There were stacks of magazines with fat, contented cats sleeping on them that you could pet without fear of being scratched. If ever there was a mystical "Ye Olde Magic Shoppe" in my life, this was it. It was a trading post for old books, and more importantly, comics. My dad would have us bring all the comics we could bear to part with, and we would watch as the clerk would shuffle through them, calculating their value. I felt as though I was in the days of the Klondike, come down from my claim in the hills and waiting for the assayer to separate the fool's gold from the real thing. His appraisal would determine how many secondhand comics we could walk away with. Always fewer than what we came in with, but my pops would pull out his wallet, careful to make sure we never left with a smaller stack. Comics were our treasure, our booty, and we would rush up to our rooms and file them away carefully on our very own spinning comic rack.

Soon, Archie, Dot, and Richie Rich gave way to Spider-Man, Captain America, X-Men, and Alpha Flight (Canada's very own superteam). Now, around this time, my memories blur a bit, but what I remember is this—I wanted to be a superhero. My brain was constantly calculating my supermoves, my supercostume, what powers I would have, how I would use them, and with whom I would share my incredible secret. My brother was in, my parents were out—lest they force me to use my newfound abilities on chores. There were, however, no radioactive spiders available to me, no toxic-waste sites, and I found out very quickly, despite my brother's urging, that jumping off the garage roof with two kites to sweep over the neighborhood didn't work. When the price of comics increased, so did my interest in girls and cars, and my treasure was relegated to the darkness of the crawlspace of our house, carefully packed in plastic bags and taped twice, not once. My desire to be a superhero, however, never abated. I couldn't help but think about how being able to fly and being bulletproof would help me in any endeavor I chose.

And then there was Joss. I met him in a small, dimly lit office, where he regaled me with tales of adventure, swashbuckling, shooting, spaceships, and narrow escapes. Um, where do I sign? He gave me a new identity, a costume, a gun, and a long brown duster for a cape. I remember that meeting so well; it was like a superhero "origin" issue. I remember Joss looking at Polaroid photos of my first costume fitting, holding up the one with the duster and gun, saying, "Action figure, anyone?"

Never in my wildest. Like some sort of superteam benefactor, Joss made superheroes out of all of us, complete with a superhideout spaceship. During filming, we'd all retreat to our dressing-room trailers and emerge like supermen with our alter egos. The boots, the suspenders, gun holstered low on my hip . . . with a flick and a spin of that wicked-awesome coat over my shoulders, I became someone else.

So, I guess the message I want to leave you with is this: What you hold in your hand is not just a comic. It is much more. It is a handbook. It is a guide. It is reference material for when you become a superhero. I have found the secret, you see. To become a superhero, all you have to do is want it badly enough, and comics are the fuel to that fire.

Incidentally, you hold in your hand my favorite (*favourite* for Canadians) . . . comic . . . ever.

Dark Horse and our cover artists have given us a great introduction to Joss's world of comic action heroes. They amazed us from the first issue, packed with shooting, crashing, punching, and splatting. Thank you, everyone. I'll be placing this series in my comic-book rack, just as soon as I get this home. It will be wrapped and double taped.

—Nathan Fillion

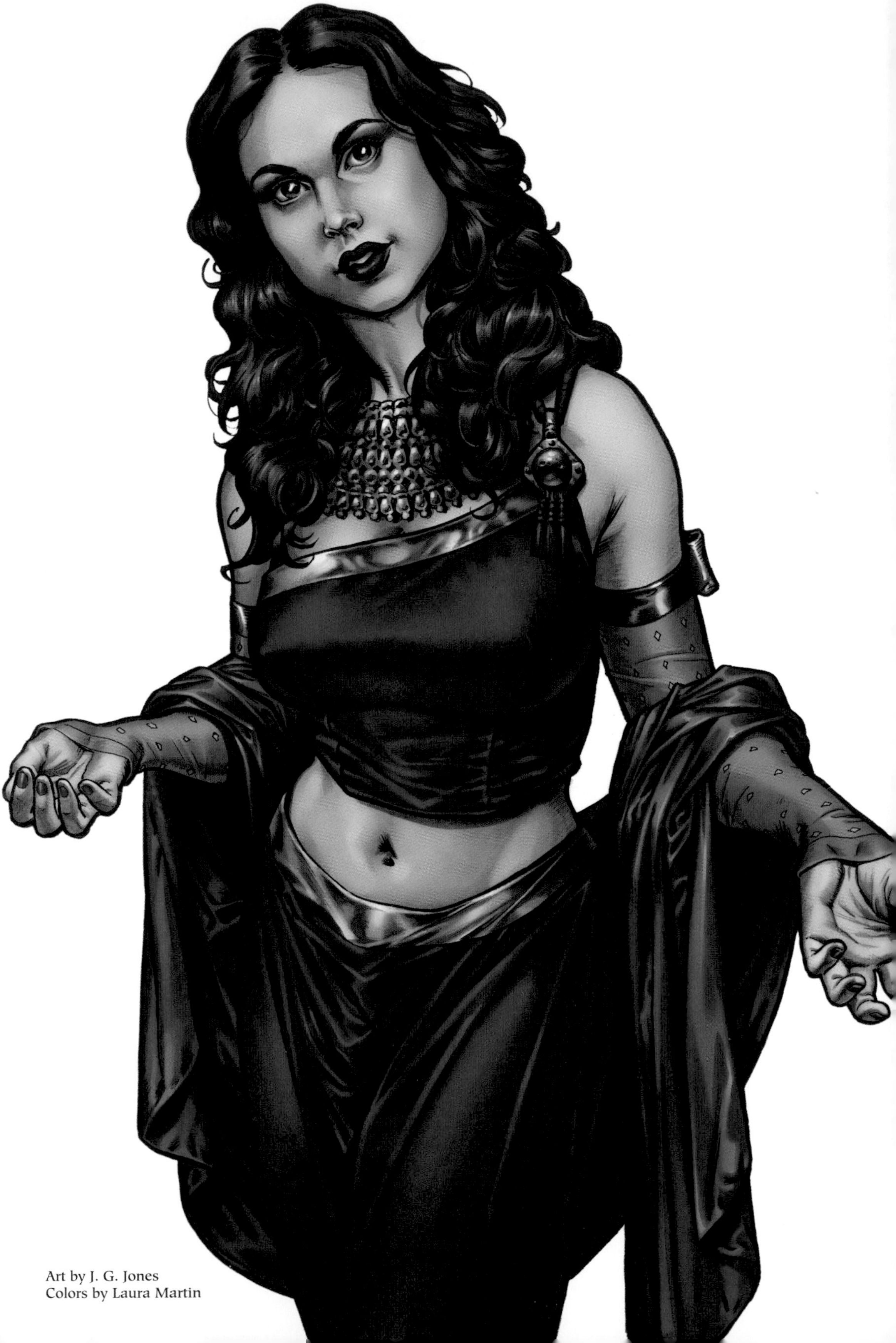

Art by J. G. Jones
Colors by Laura Martin

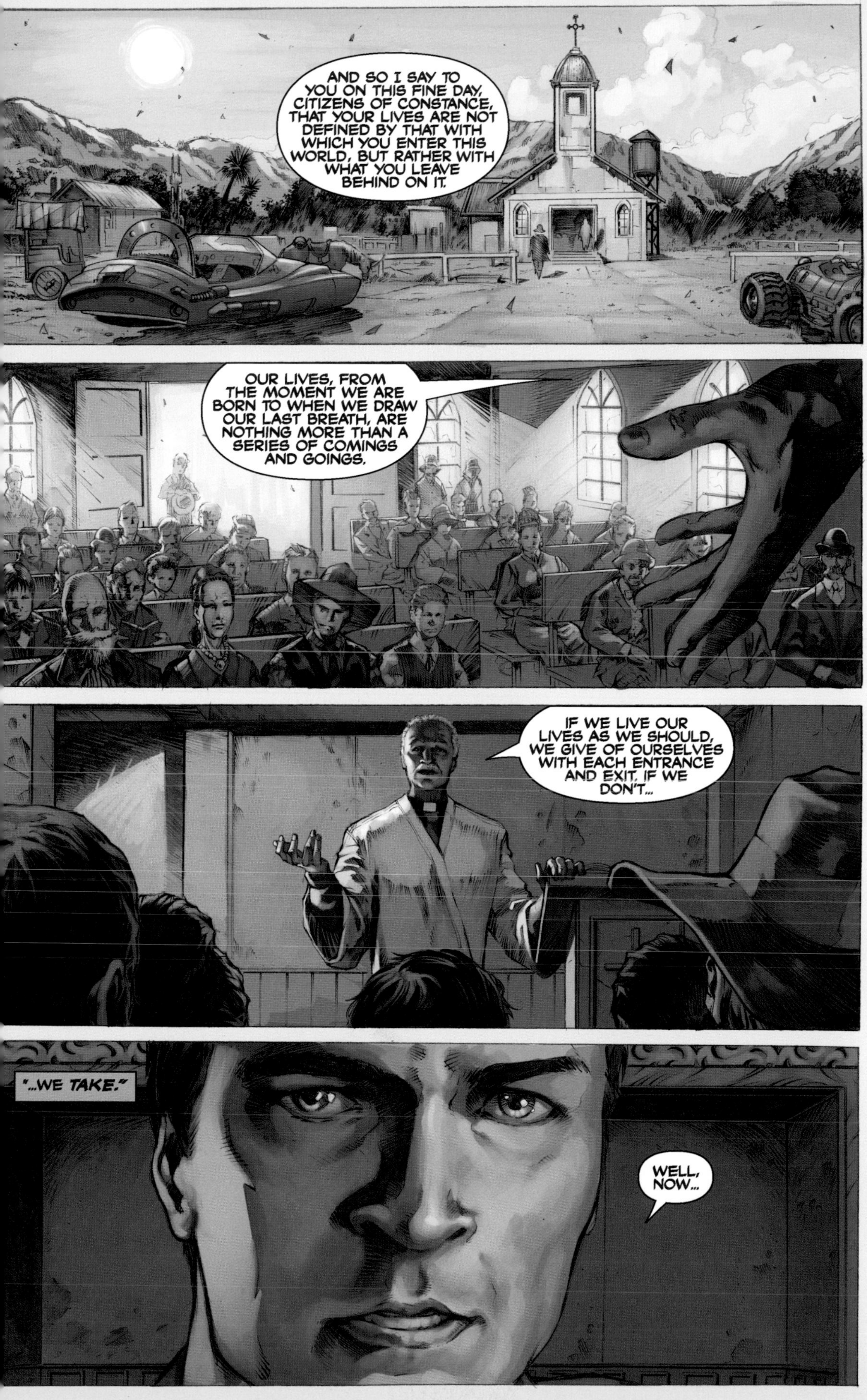
AND SO I SAY TO YOU ON THIS FINE DAY, CITIZENS OF CONSTANCE, THAT YOUR LIVES ARE NOT DEFINED BY THAT WITH WHICH YOU ENTER THIS WORLD, BUT RATHER WITH WHAT YOU LEAVE BEHIND ON IT.
OUR LIVES, FROM THE MOMENT WE ARE BORN TO WHEN WE DRAW OUR LAST BREATH, ARE NOTHING MORE THAN A SERIES OF COMINGS AND GOINGS.
IF WE LIVE OUR LIVES AS WE SHOULD, WE GIVE OF OURSELVES WITH EACH ENTRANCE AND EXIT. IF WE DON'T...
"...WE TAKE."
WELL, NOW...

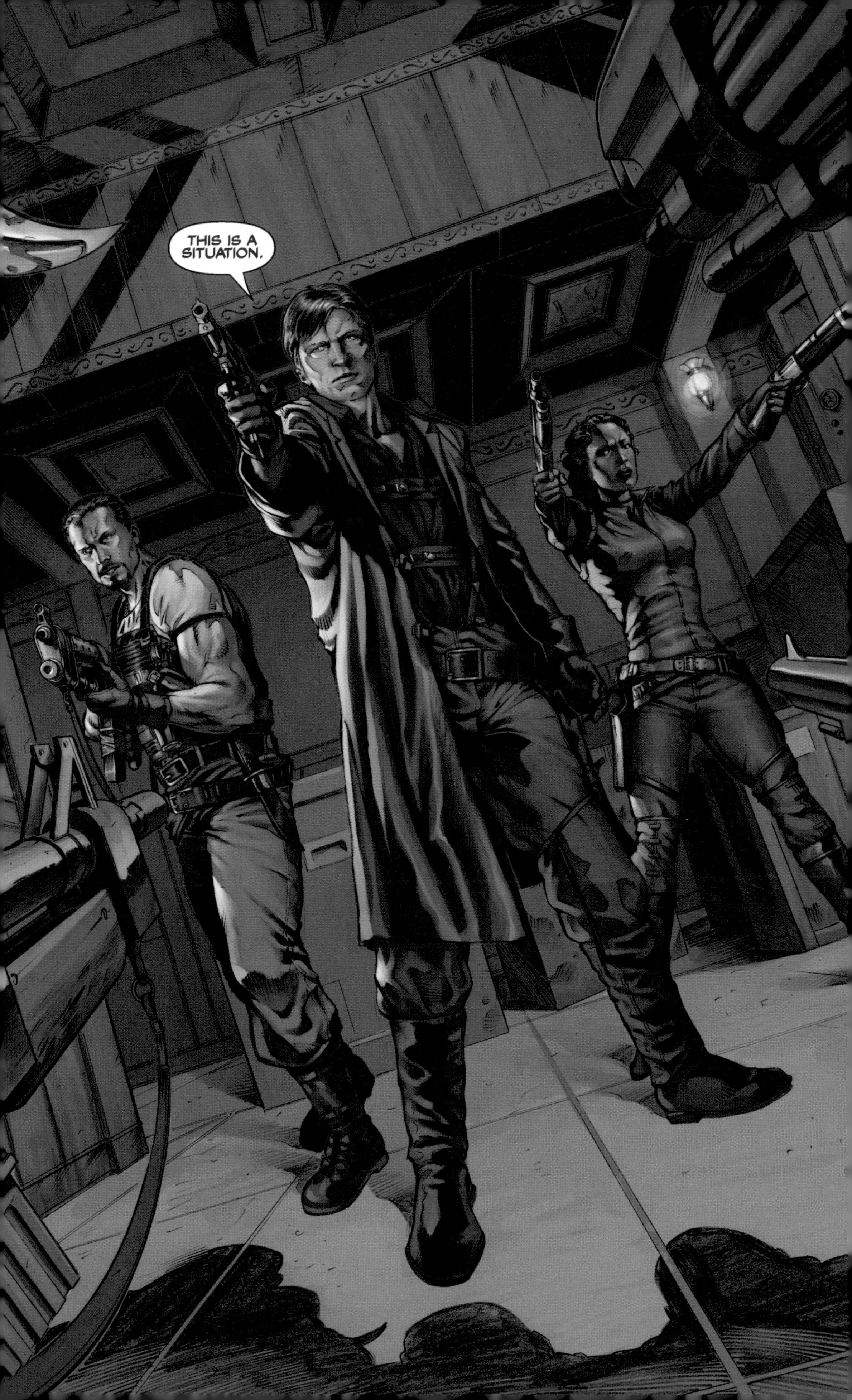
THIS IS A SITUATION.

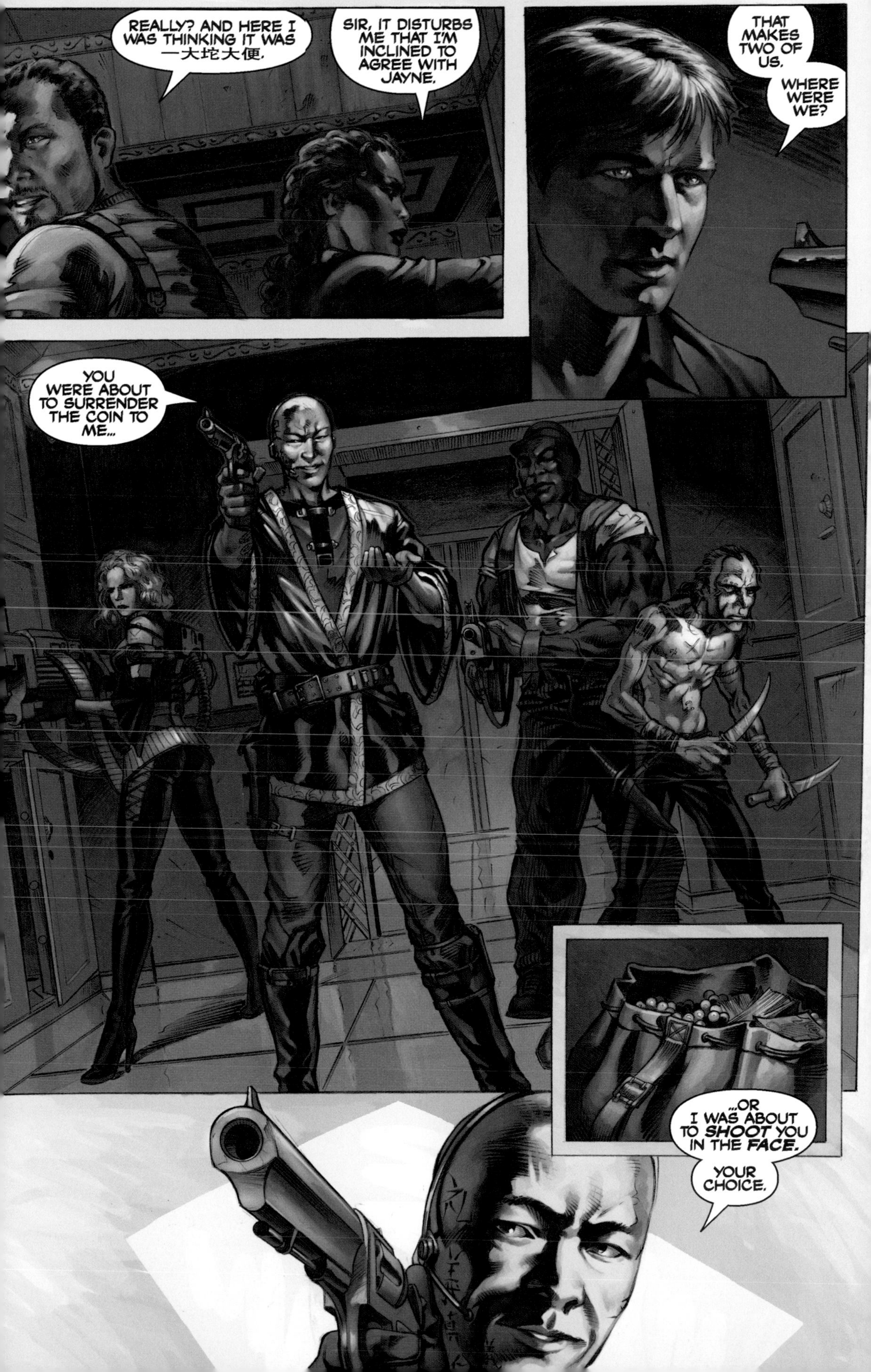
REALLY? AND HERE I WAS THINKING IT WAS 一大坨大便.
SIR, IT DISTURBS ME THAT I'M INCLINED TO AGREE WITH JAYNE.
THAT MAKES TWO OF US.
WHERE WERE WE?
YOU WERE ABOUT TO SURRENDER THE COIN TO ME...
...OR I WAS ABOUT TO *SHOOT* YOU IN THE *FACE.*
YOUR CHOICE.

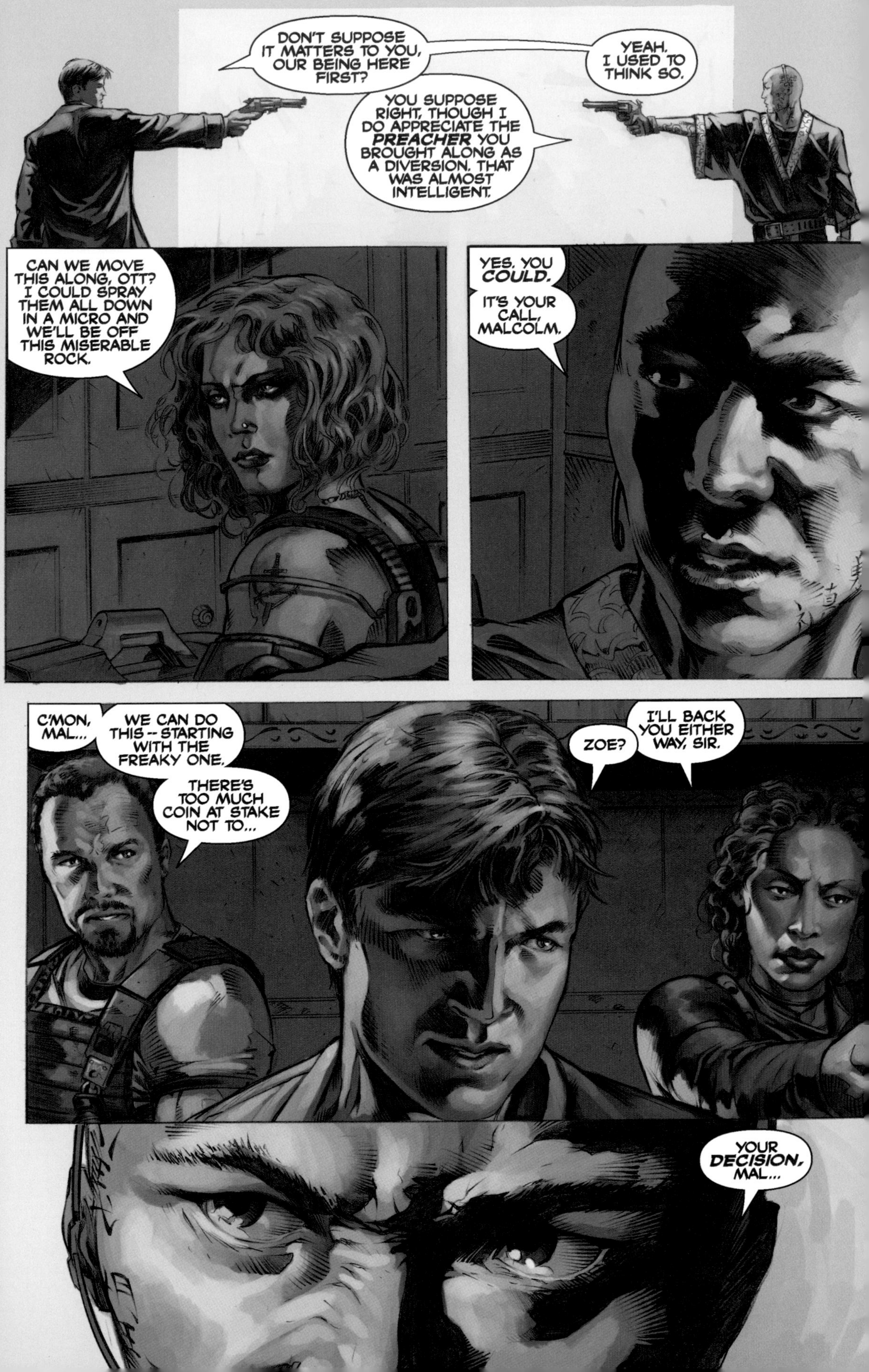
DON'T SUPPOSE IT MATTERS TO YOU, OUR BEING HERE FIRST?
YEAH. I USED TO THINK SO.
YOU SUPPOSE RIGHT, THOUGH I DO APPRECIATE THE PREACHER YOU BROUGHT ALONG AS A DIVERSION. THAT WAS ALMOST INTELLIGENT.
CAN WE MOVE THIS ALONG, OTT? I COULD SPRAY THEM ALL DOWN IN A MICRO AND WE'LL BE OFF THIS MISERABLE ROCK.
YES, YOU COULD.
IT'S YOUR CALL, MALCOLM.
C'MON, MAL...
WE CAN DO THIS -- STARTING WITH THE FREAKY ONE.
THERE'S TOO MUCH COIN AT STAKE NOT TO...
ZOE?
I'LL BACK YOU EITHER WAY, SIR.
YOUR DECISION, MAL...

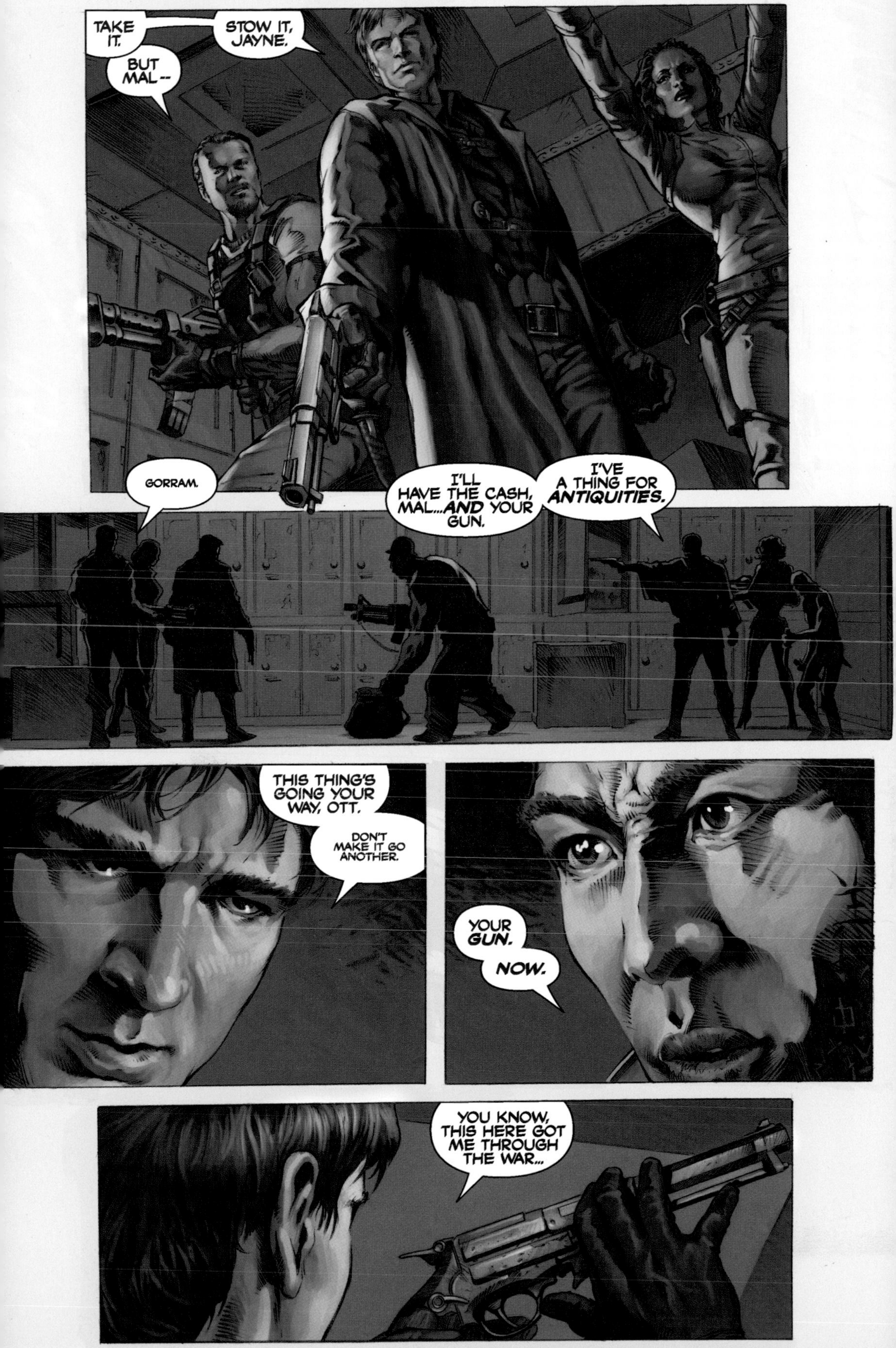

TAKE IT.
BUT MAL--
STOW IT, JAYNE.
GORRAM.
I'LL HAVE THE CASH, MAL...AND YOUR GUN.
I'VE A THING FOR ANTIQUITIES.
THIS THING'S GOING YOUR WAY, OTT.
DON'T MAKE IT GO ANOTHER.
YOUR GUN.
NOW.
YOU KNOW, THIS HERE GOT ME THROUGH THE WAR...

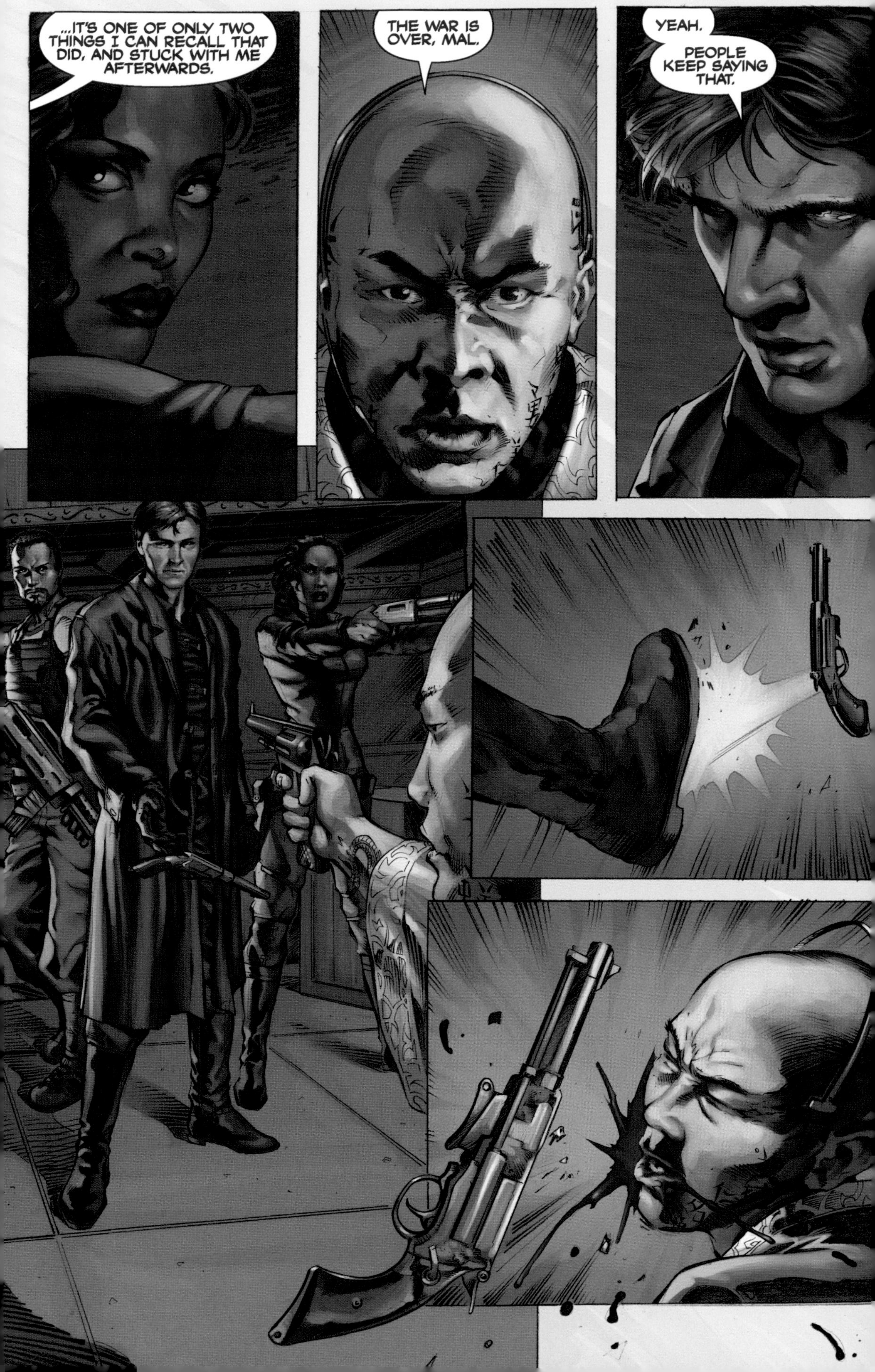
...IT'S ONE OF ONLY TWO THINGS I CAN RECALL THAT DID, AND STUCK WITH ME AFTERWARDS.
THE WAR IS OVER, MAL.
YEAH.
PEOPLE KEEP SAYING THAT.

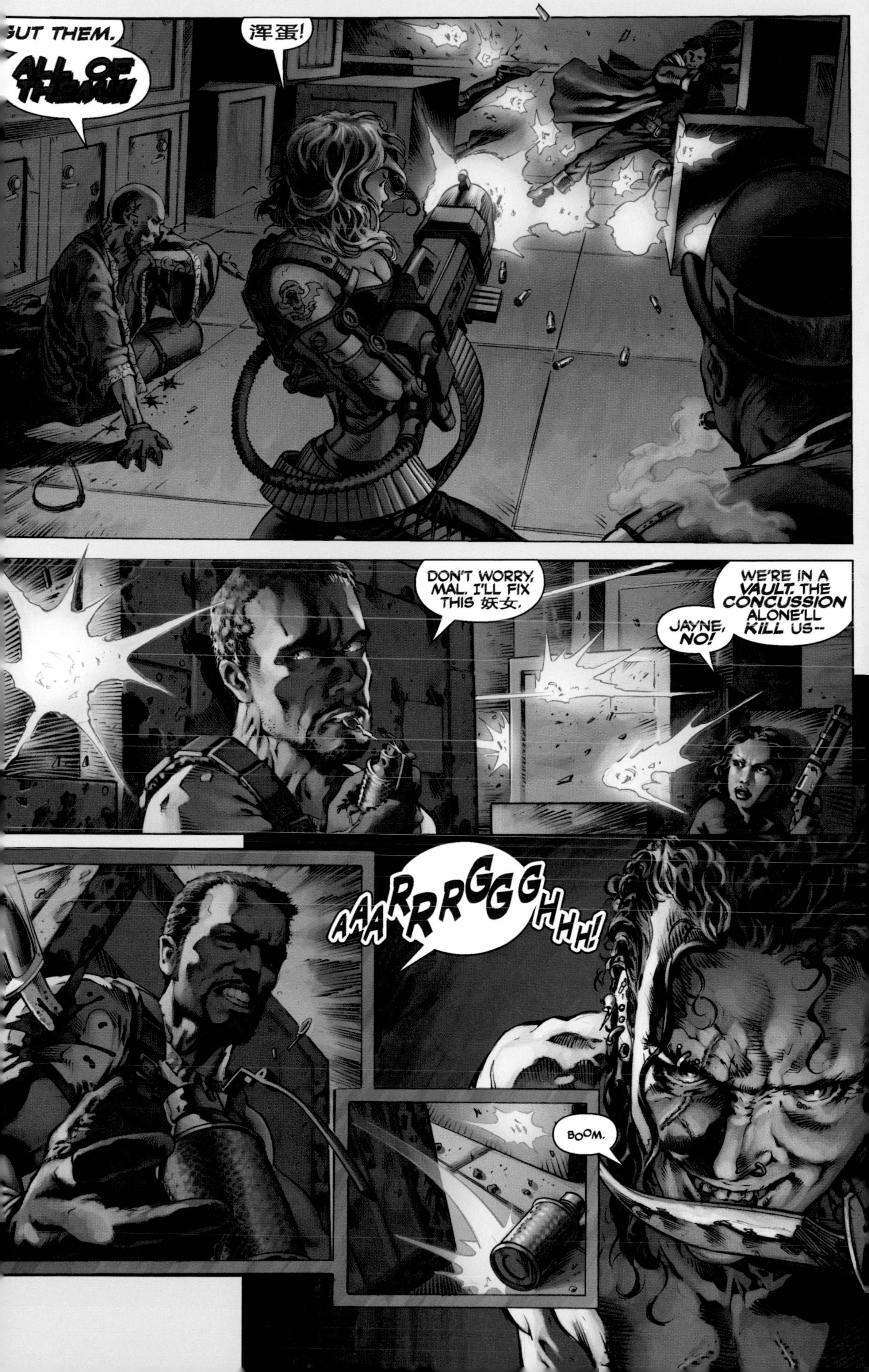
GUT THEM.
ALL OF THEM
浑蛋!
DON'T WORRY, MAL, I'LL FIX THIS 妖女.
JAYNE, NO!
WE'RE IN A VAULT. THE CONCUSSION ALONE'LL KILL US--
AAARRRGGGHHH!
BOOM.

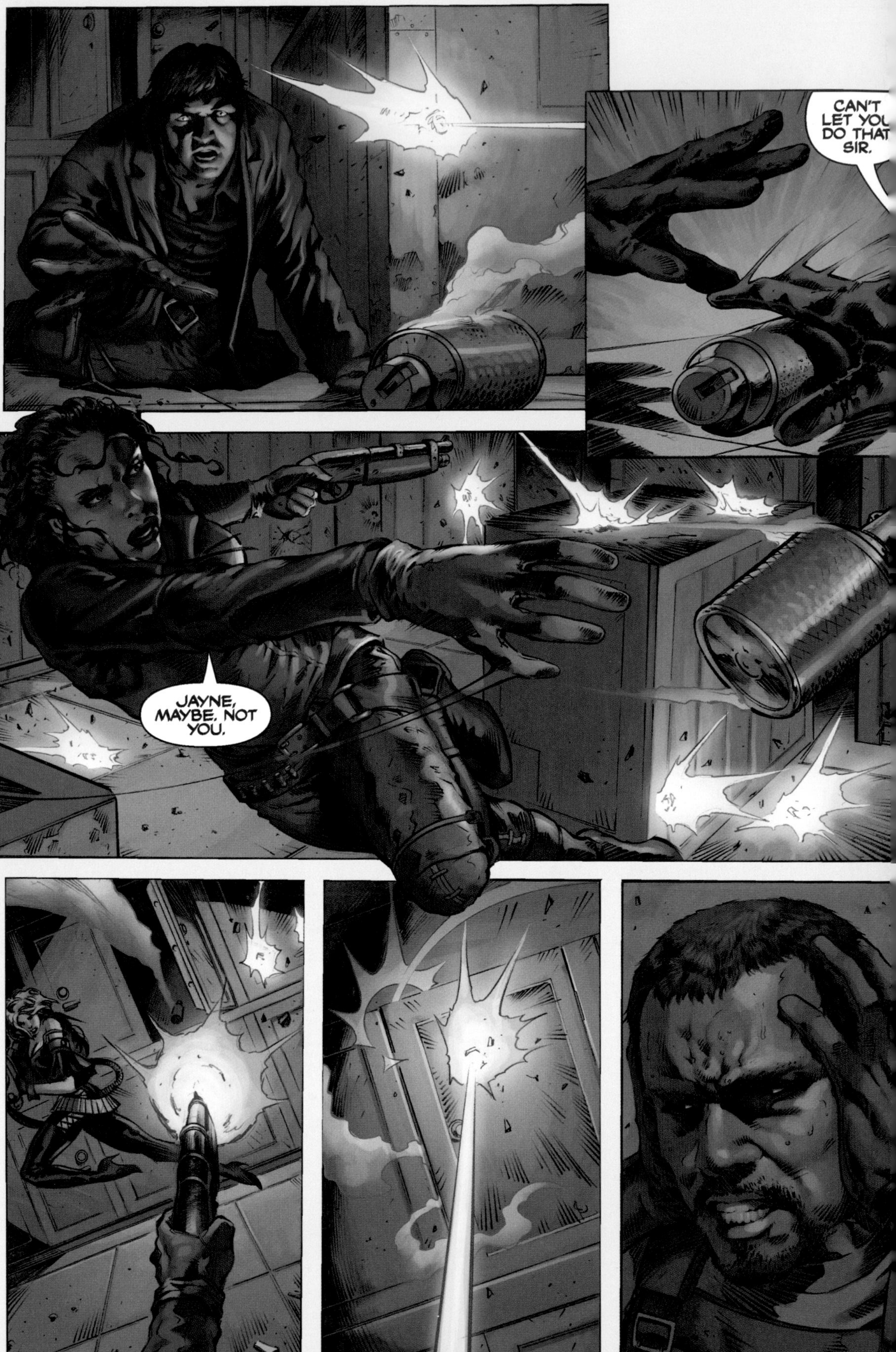
CAN'T LET YOU DO THAT SIR.
JAYNE, MAYBE. NOT YOU.

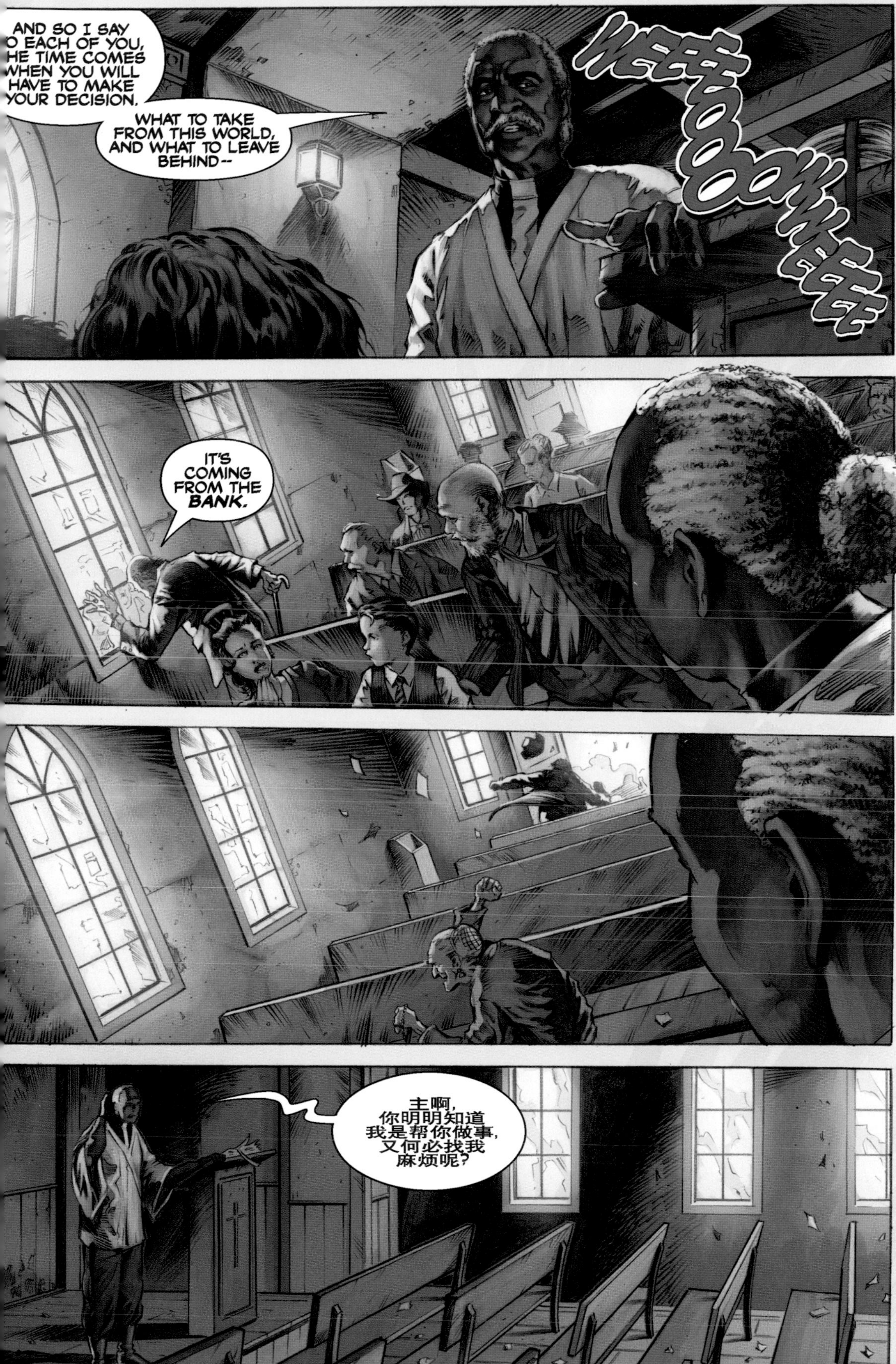
AND SO I SAY
O EACH OF YOU,
HE TIME COMES
WHEN YOU WILL
HAVE TO MAKE
YOUR DECISION.
WHAT TO TAKE FROM THIS WORLD, AND WHAT TO LEAVE BEHIND--
WEEEEOOOOWEEEE
IT'S COMING FROM THE *BANK.*
主啊，你明明知道我是帮你做事，又何必找我麻烦呢？

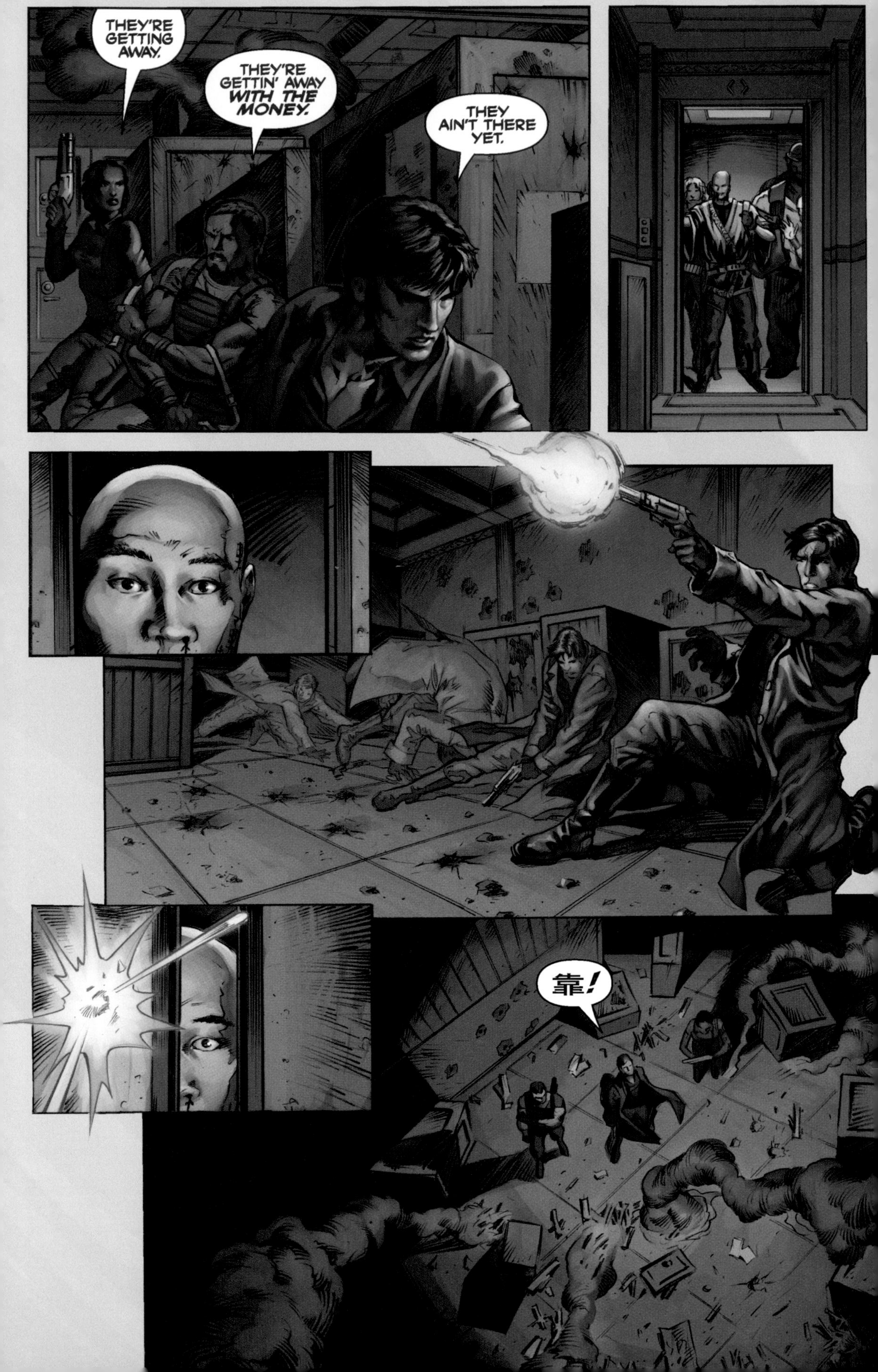
THEY'RE GETTING AWAY.
THEY'RE GETTIN' AWAY WITH THE MONEY.
THEY AIN'T THERE YET.
靠!

GONNA TAKE A WHILE FOR THE STINK OF THIS TO PASS.

JUST A SEWER, JAYNE.

WEREN'T TALKING ABOUT THE SEWER.

NOW AIN'T THE TIME, JAYNE.

UNDERSTOOD?

WELL, YOU JUST BE SURE AND SAY *WHEN.*

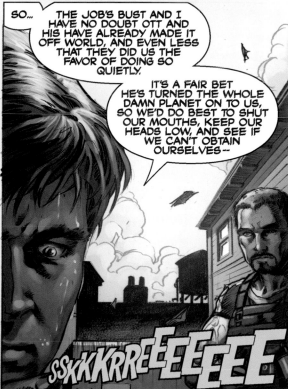

SO...

THE JOB'S BUST AND I HAVE NO DOUBT OTT AND HIS HAVE ALREADY MADE IT OFF WORLD, AND EVEN LESS THAT THEY DID US THE FAVOR OF DOING SO QUIETLY.

IT'S A FAIR BET HE'S TURNED THE WHOLE DAMN PLANET ON TO US, SO WE'D DO BEST TO SHUT OUR MOUTHS, KEEP OUR HEADS LOW, AND SEE IF WE CAN'T OBTAIN OURSELVES--

SSKKKRREEEEEEE

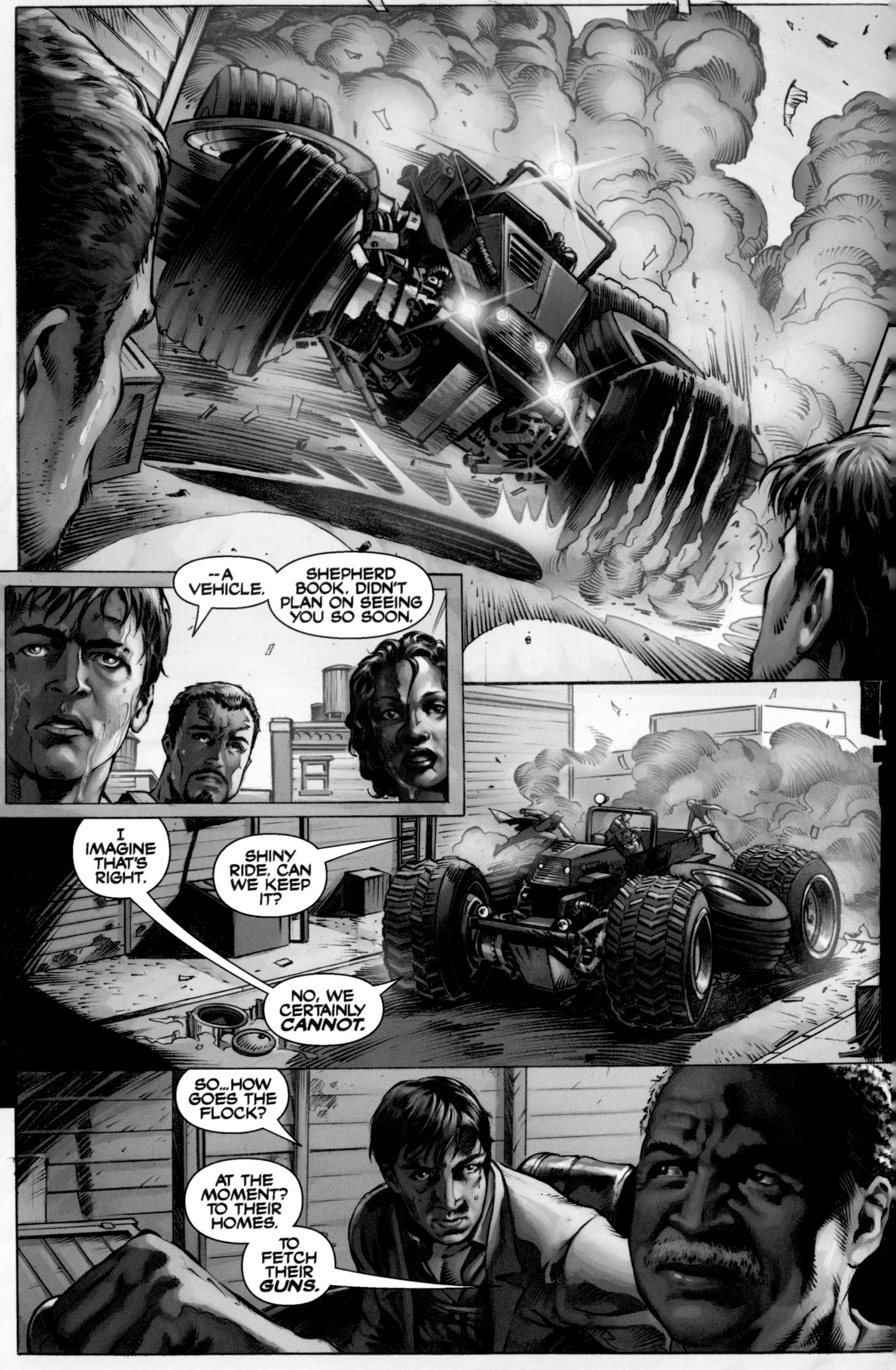
--A VEHICLE.
SHEPHERD BOOK. DIDN'T PLAN ON SEEING YOU SO SOON.
I IMAGINE THAT'S RIGHT.
SHINY RIDE. CAN WE KEEP IT?
NO, WE CERTAINLY *CANNOT.*
SO...HOW GOES THE FLOCK?
AT THE MOMENT? TO THEIR HOMES.
TO FETCH THEIR *GUNS.*

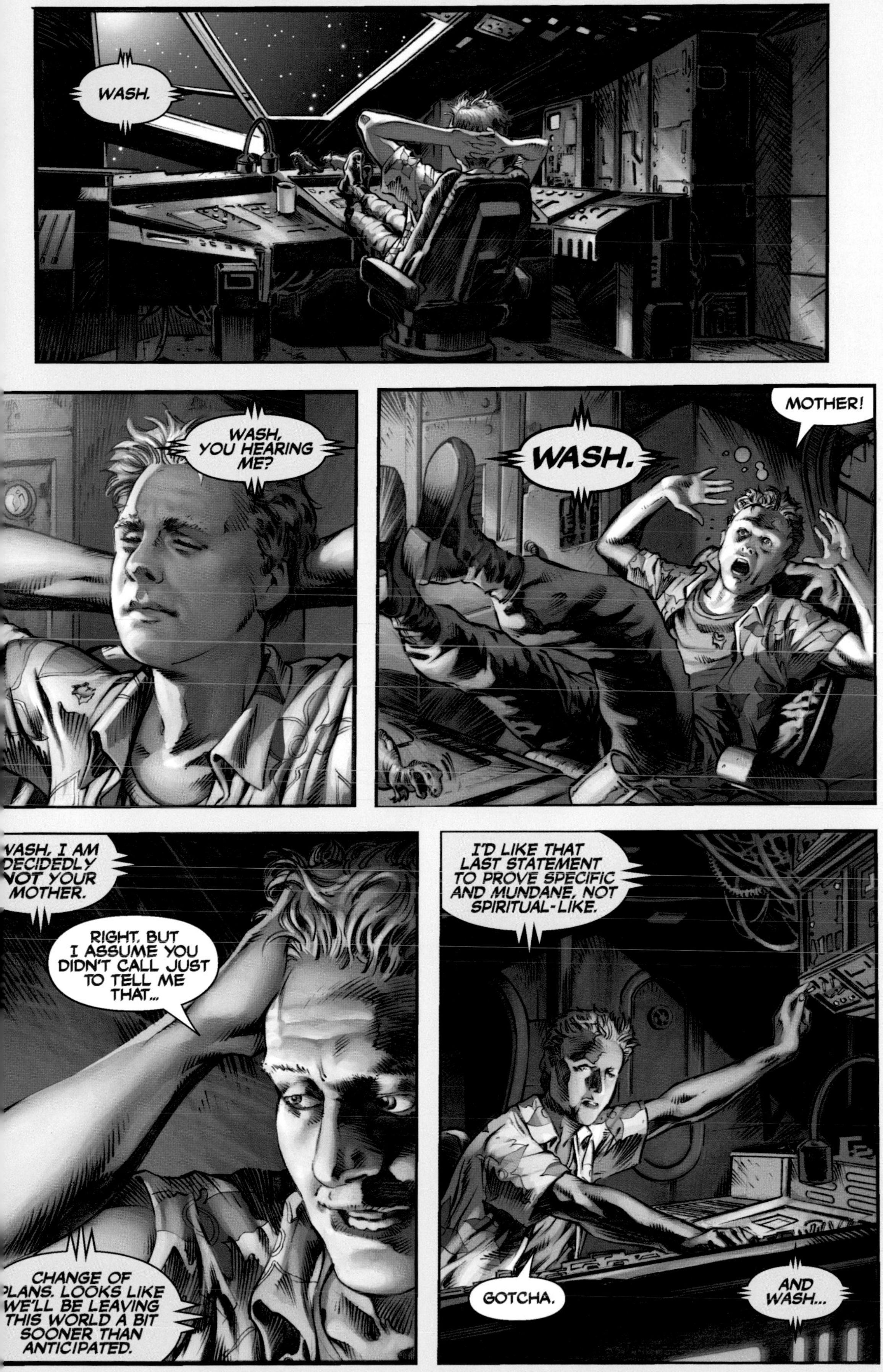
WASH.
WASH, YOU HEARING ME?
WASH.
MOTHER!
WASH, I AM DECIDEDLY NOT YOUR MOTHER.
RIGHT, BUT I ASSUME YOU DIDN'T CALL JUST TO TELL ME THAT...
CHANGE OF PLANS. LOOKS LIKE WE'LL BE LEAVING THIS WORLD A BIT SOONER THAN ANTICIPATED.
I'D LIKE THAT LAST STATEMENT TO PROVE SPECIFIC AND MUNDANE, NOT SPIRITUAL-LIKE.
GOTCHA.
AND WASH...

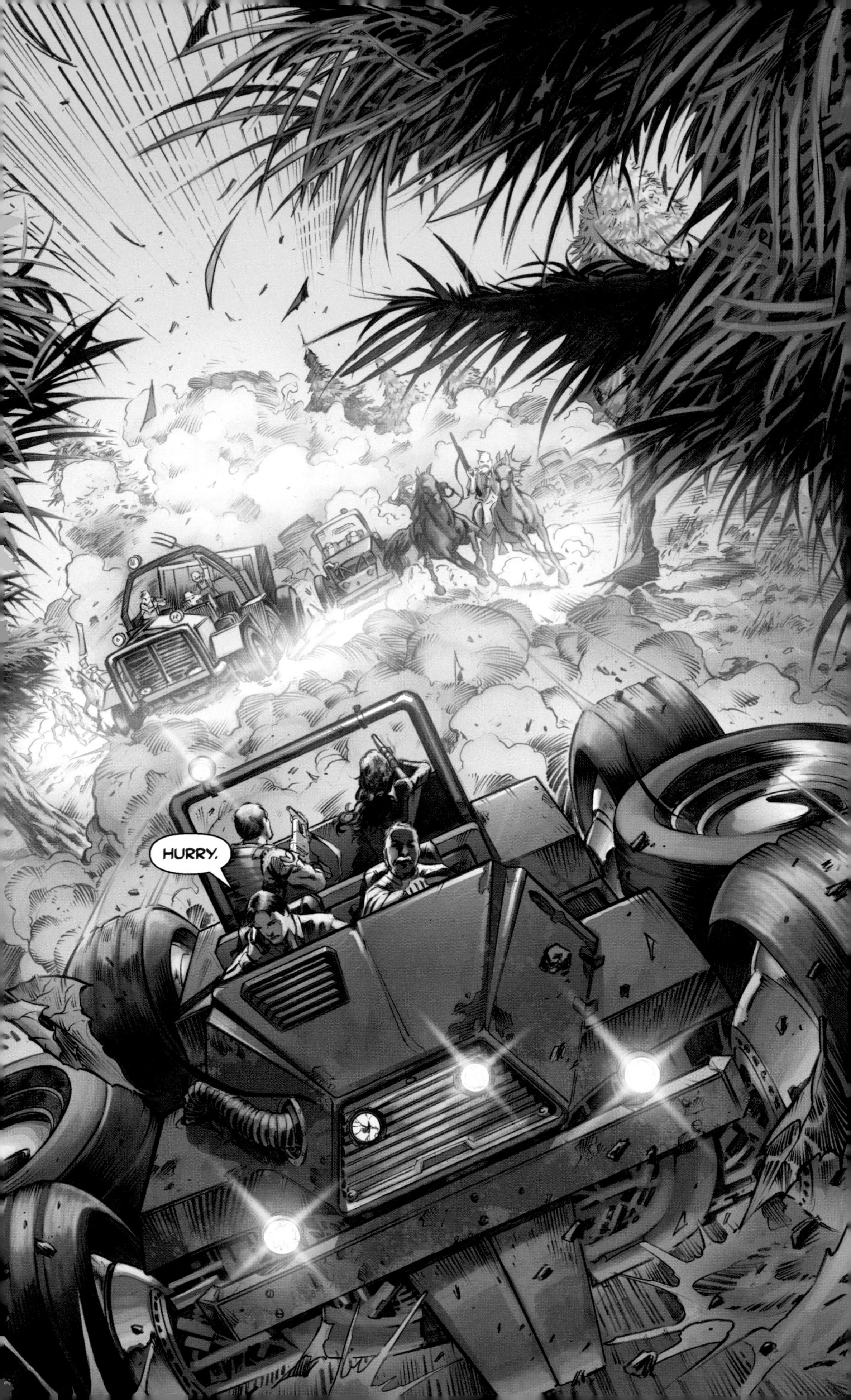
HURRY.

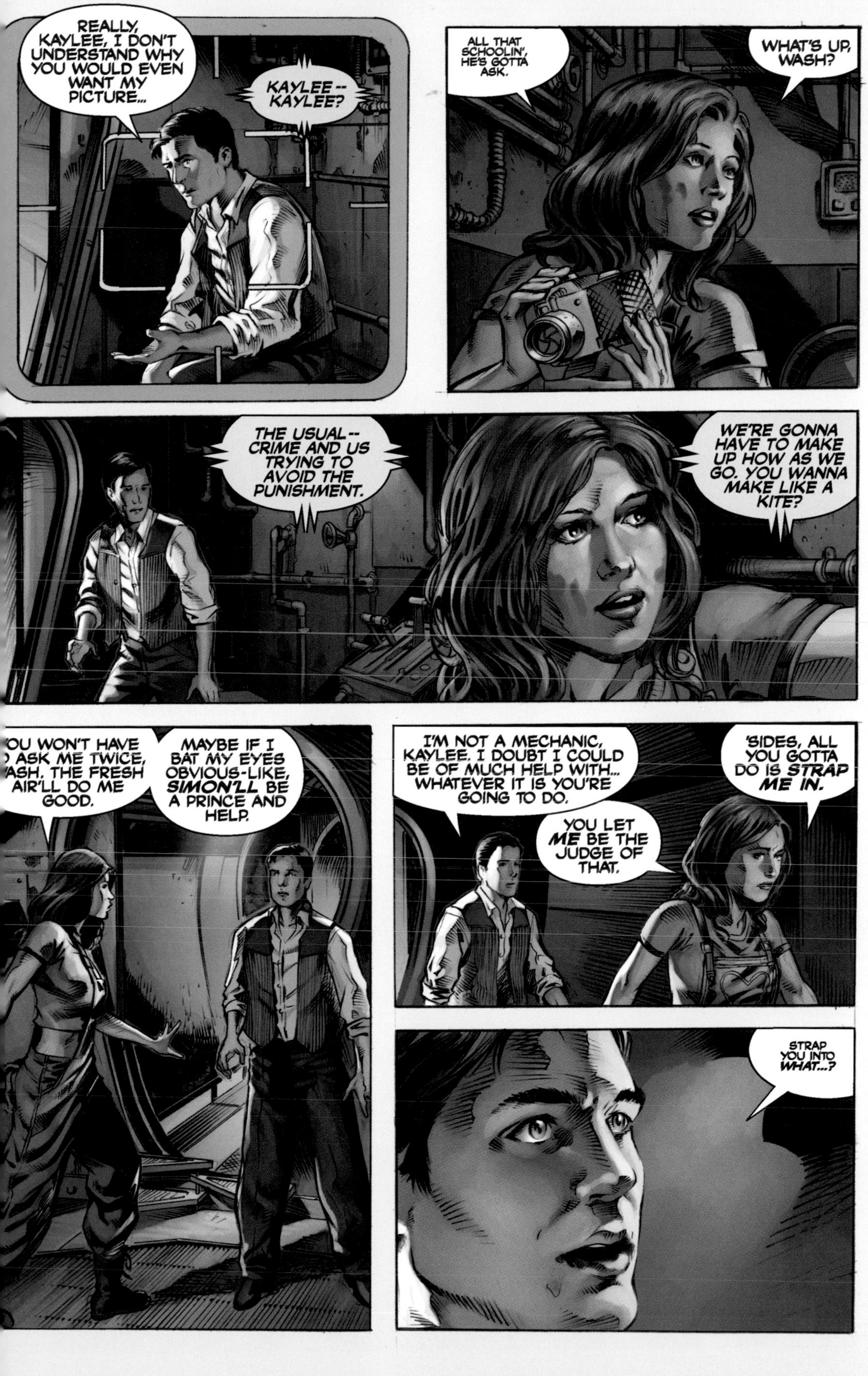
REALLY, KAYLEE, I DON'T UNDERSTAND WHY YOU WOULD EVEN WANT MY PICTURE...
KAYLEE -- KAYLEE?
ALL THAT SCHOOLIN', HE'S GOTTA ASK.
WHAT'S UP, WASH?
THE USUAL-- CRIME AND US TRYING TO AVOID THE PUNISHMENT.
WE'RE GONNA HAVE TO MAKE UP HOW AS WE GO. YOU WANNA MAKE LIKE A KITE?
OU WON'T HAVE ASK ME TWICE, ASH. THE FRESH AIR'LL DO ME GOOD.
MAYBE IF I BAT MY EYES OBVIOUS-LIKE, SIMON'LL BE A PRINCE AND HELP.
I'M NOT A MECHANIC, KAYLEE. I DOUBT I COULD BE OF MUCH HELP WITH... WHATEVER IT IS YOU'RE GOING TO DO.
YOU LET ME BE THE JUDGE OF THAT.
'SIDES, ALL YOU GOTTA DO IS STRAP ME IN.
STRAP YOU INTO WHAT...?

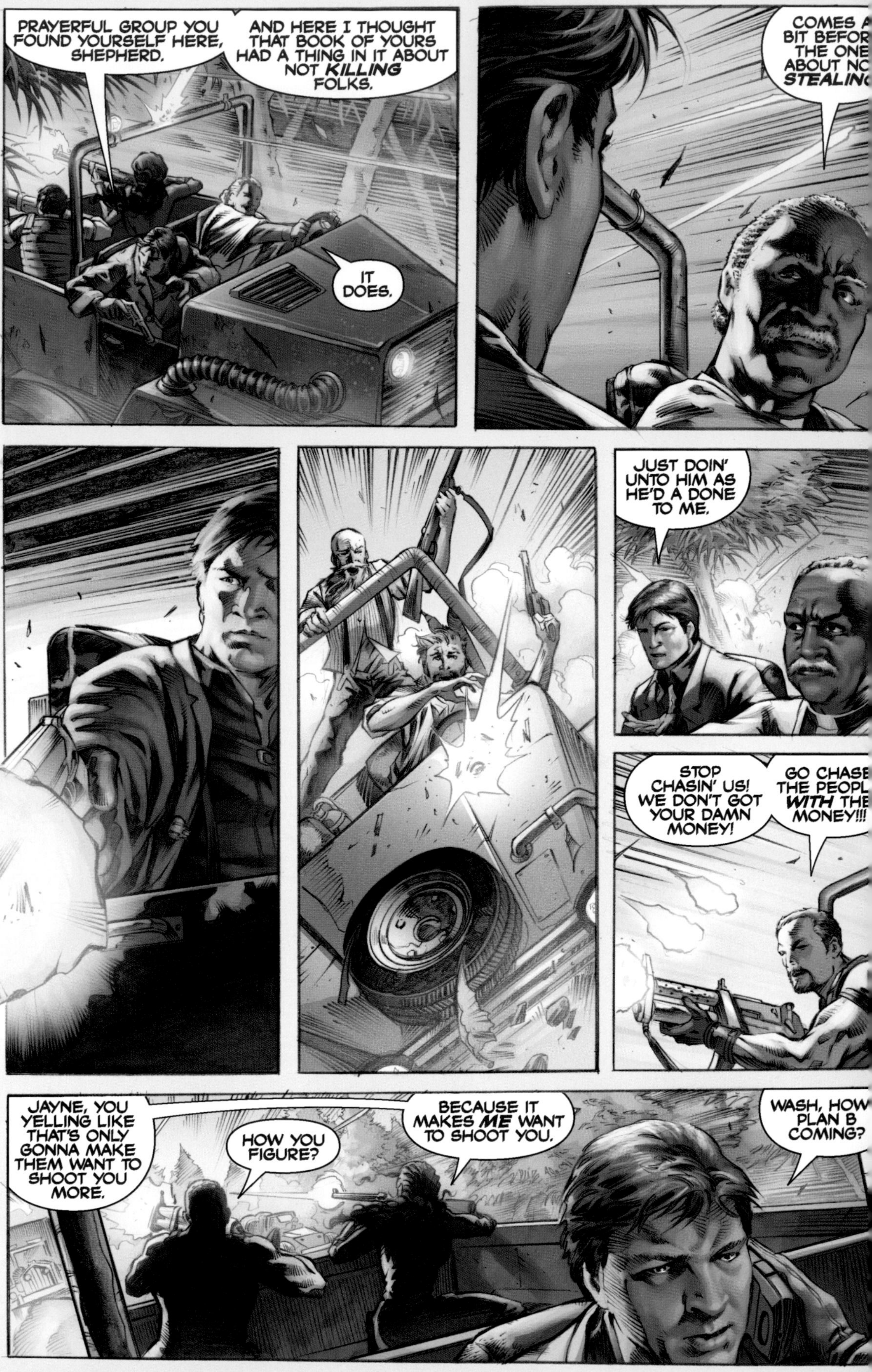
PRAYERFUL GROUP YOU FOUND YOURSELF HERE, SHEPHERD.
AND HERE I THOUGHT THAT BOOK OF YOURS HAD A THING IN IT ABOUT NOT *KILLING* FOLKS.
IT DOES.
COMES A BIT BEFOR THE ONE ABOUT NO *STEALIN*
JUST DOIN' UNTO HIM AS HE'D A DONE TO ME.
STOP CHASIN' US! WE DON'T GOT YOUR DAMN MONEY!
GO CHASE THE PEOPL *WITH* THE MONEY!!!
JAYNE, YOU YELLING LIKE THAT'S ONLY GONNA MAKE THEM WANT TO SHOOT YOU MORE.
HOW YOU FIGURE?
BECAUSE IT MAKES *ME* WANT TO SHOOT YOU.
WASH, HOW PLAN B COMING?

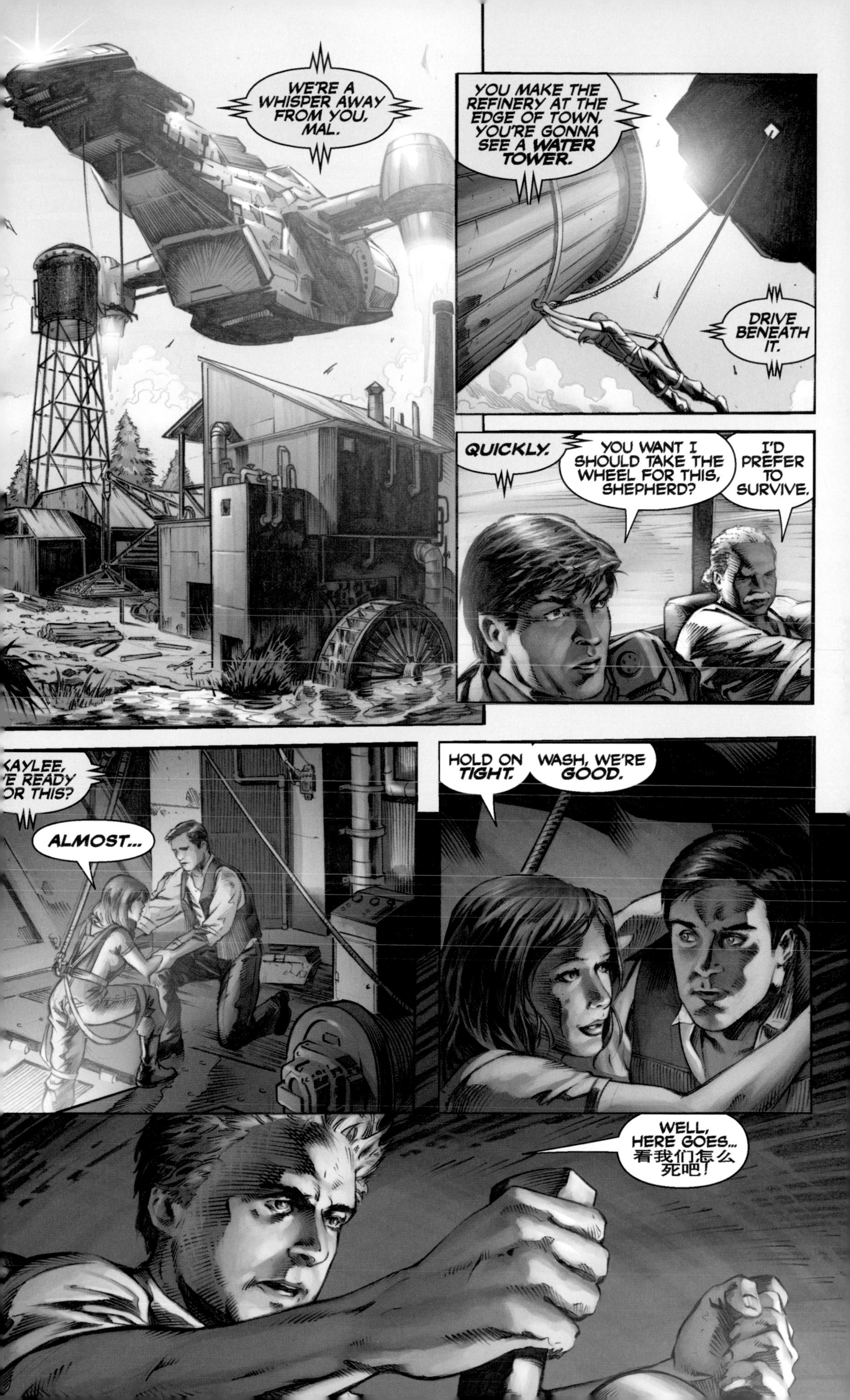
WE'RE A WHISPER AWAY FROM YOU, MAL.
YOU MAKE THE REFINERY AT THE EDGE OF TOWN, YOU'RE GONNA SEE A WATER TOWER.
DRIVE BENEATH IT.
QUICKLY.
YOU WANT I SHOULD TAKE THE WHEEL FOR THIS, SHEPHERD?
I'D PREFER TO SURVIVE.
KAYLEE, 'E READY OR THIS?
ALMOST...
HOLD ON TIGHT.
WASH, WE'RE GOOD.
WELL, HERE GOES... 看我们怎么死吧!

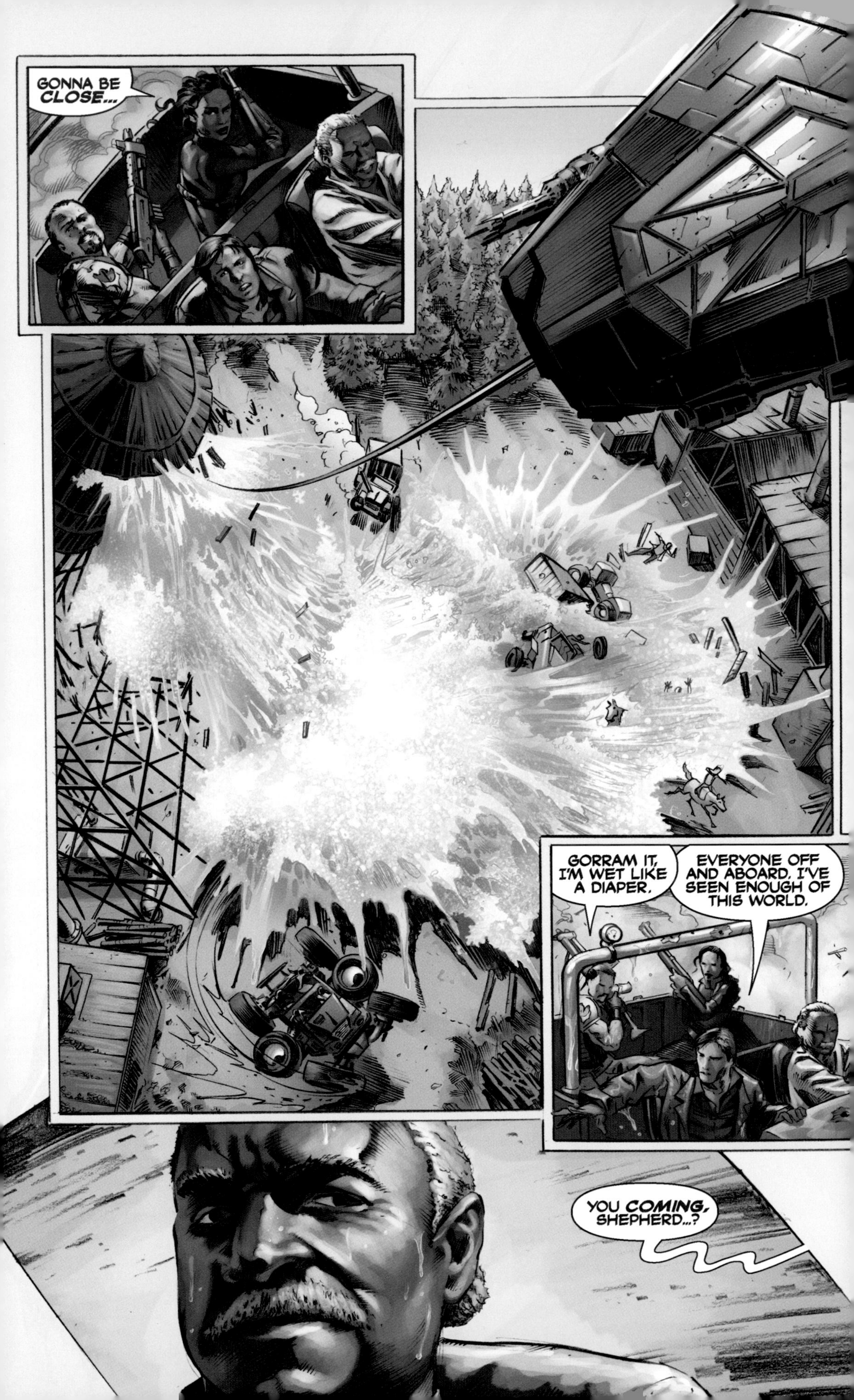
GONNA BE CLOSE...
GORRAM IT, I'M WET LIKE A DIAPER.
EVERYONE OFF AND ABOARD. I'VE SEEN ENOUGH OF THIS WORLD.
YOU COMING, SHEPHERD...?

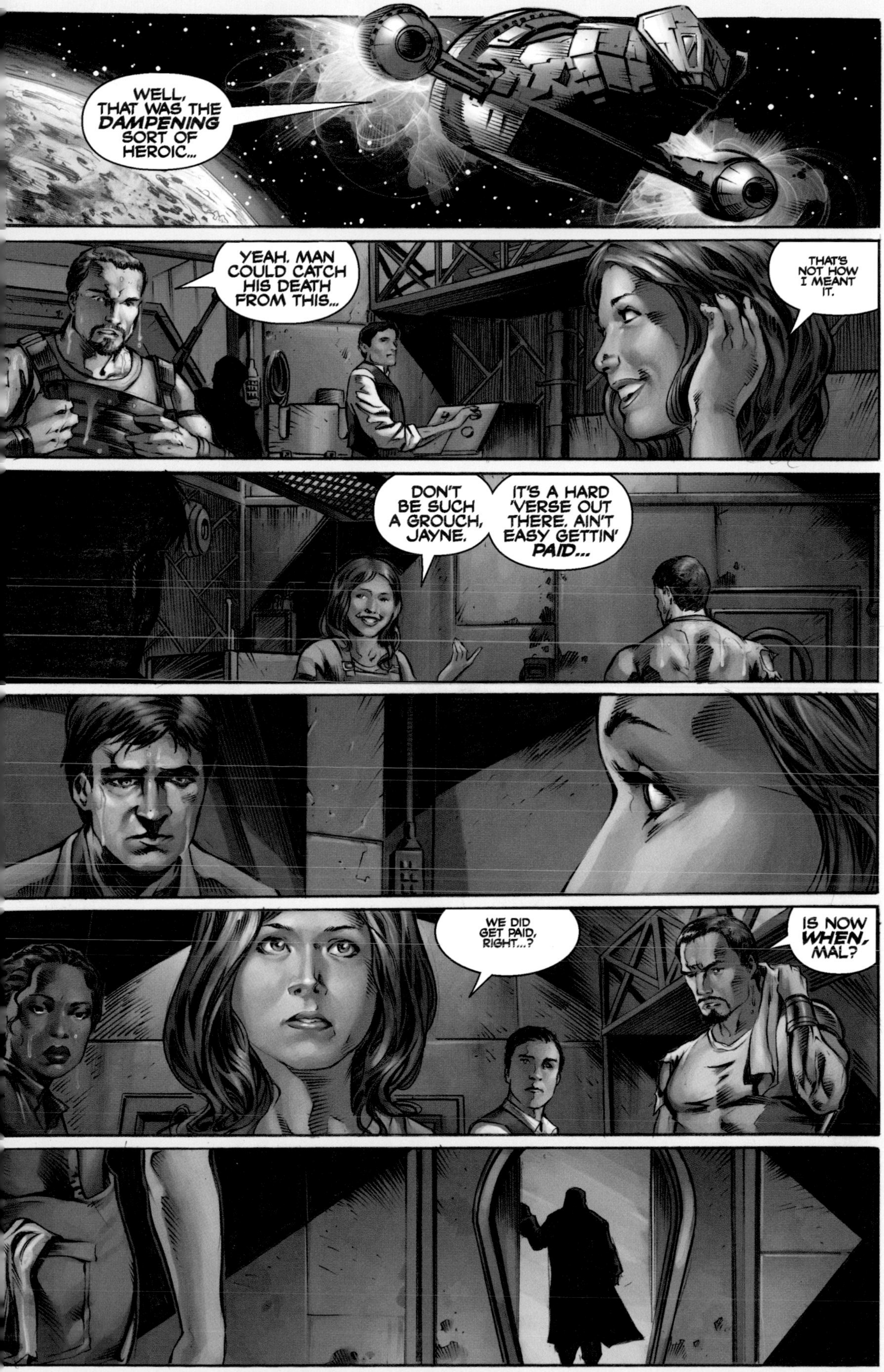
WELL, THAT WAS THE DAMPENING SORT OF HEROIC...
YEAH. MAN COULD CATCH HIS DEATH FROM THIS...
THAT'S NOT HOW I MEANT IT.
DON'T BE SUCH A GROUCH, JAYNE.
IT'S A HARD 'VERSE OUT THERE. AIN'T EASY GETTIN' PAID...
WE DID GET PAID, RIGHT...?
IS NOW WHEN, MAL?

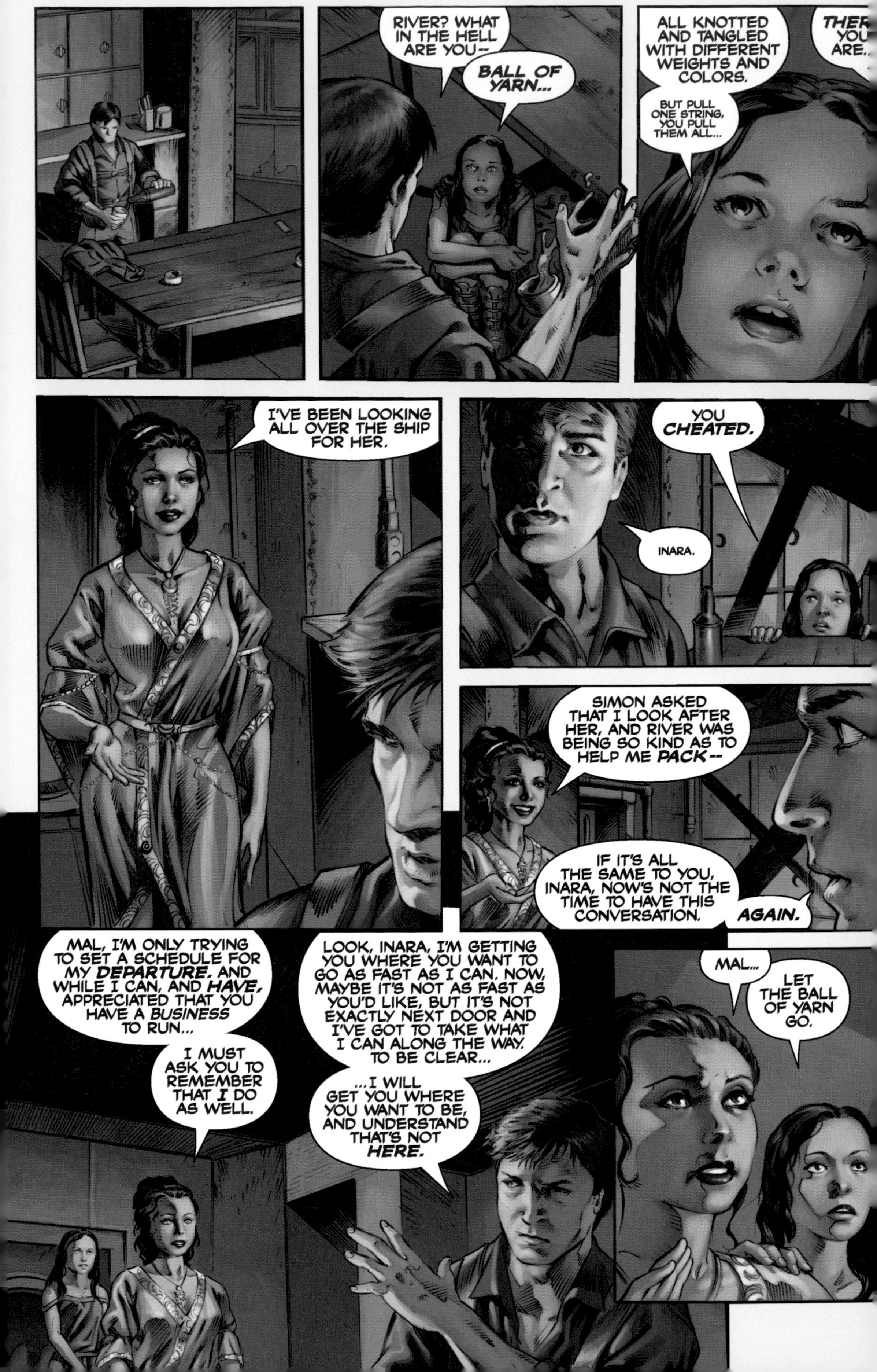
RIVER? WHAT IN THE HELL ARE YOU--
BALL OF YARN...
ALL KNOTTED AND TANGLED WITH DIFFERENT WEIGHTS AND COLORS.
BUT PULL ONE STRING, YOU PULL THEM ALL...
THERE YOU ARE...
I'VE BEEN LOOKING ALL OVER THE SHIP FOR HER.
YOU CHEATED.
INARA.
SIMON ASKED THAT I LOOK AFTER HER, AND RIVER WAS BEING SO KIND AS TO HELP ME PACK--
IF IT'S ALL THE SAME TO YOU, INARA, NOW'S NOT THE TIME TO HAVE THIS CONVERSATION.
AGAIN.
MAL, I'M ONLY TRYING TO SET A SCHEDULE FOR MY DEPARTURE. AND WHILE I CAN, AND HAVE, APPRECIATED THAT YOU HAVE A BUSINESS TO RUN...
I MUST ASK YOU TO REMEMBER THAT I DO AS WELL.
LOOK, INARA, I'M GETTING YOU WHERE YOU WANT TO GO AS FAST AS I CAN. NOW, MAYBE IT'S NOT AS FAST AS YOU'D LIKE, BUT IT'S NOT EXACTLY NEXT DOOR AND I'VE GOT TO TAKE WHAT I CAN ALONG THE WAY. TO BE CLEAR...
...I WILL GET YOU WHERE YOU WANT TO BE, AND UNDERSTAND THAT'S NOT HERE.
MAL...
LET THE BALL OF YARN GO.

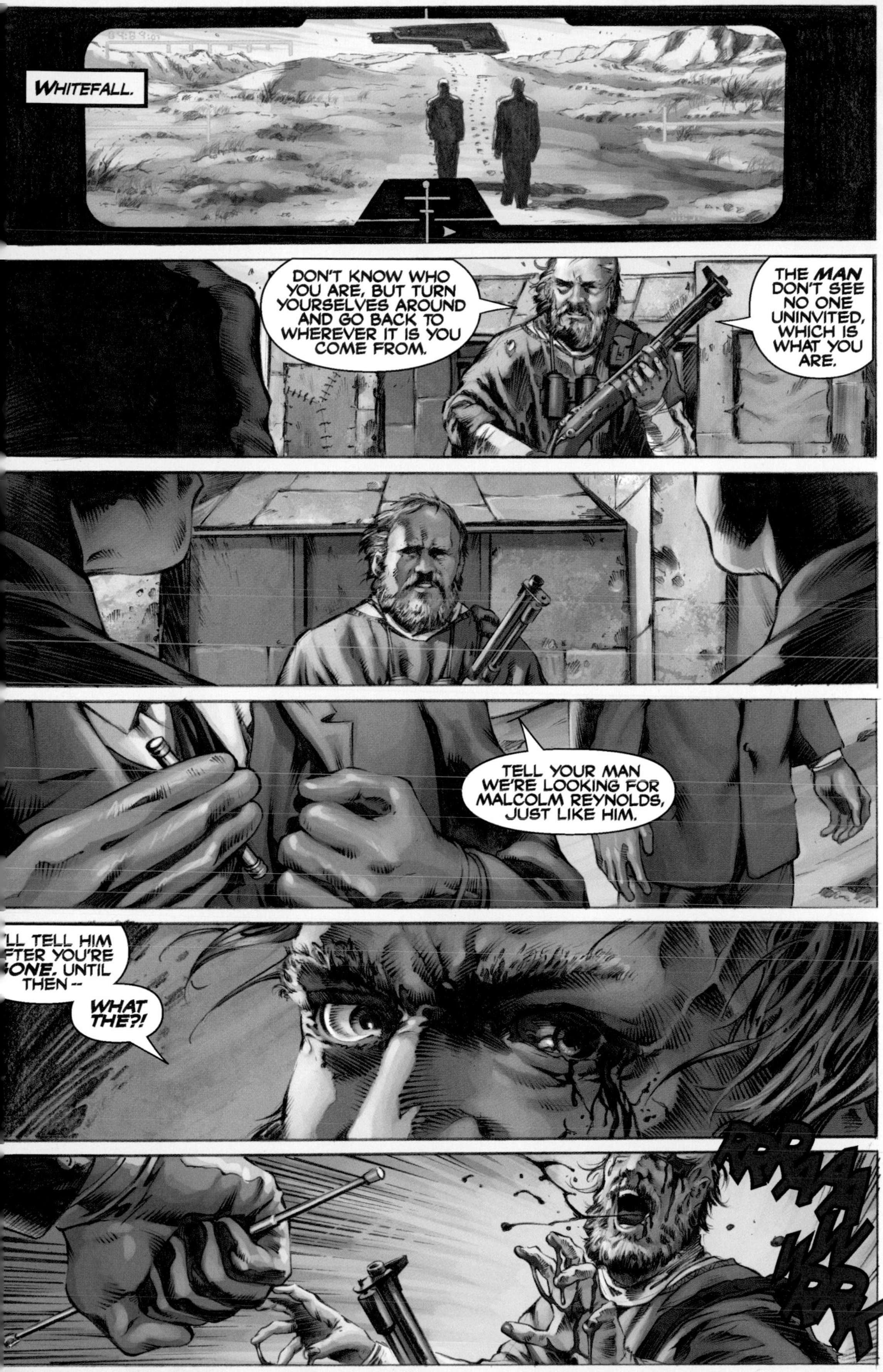
WHITEFALL.
DON'T KNOW WHO YOU ARE, BUT TURN YOURSELVES AROUND AND GO BACK TO WHEREVER IT IS YOU COME FROM.
THE MAN DON'T SEE NO ONE UNINVITED, WHICH IS WHAT YOU ARE.
TELL YOUR MAN WE'RE LOOKING FOR MALCOLM REYNOLDS, JUST LIKE HIM.
'LL TELL HIM FTER YOU'RE GONE. UNTIL THEN --
WHAT THE?!

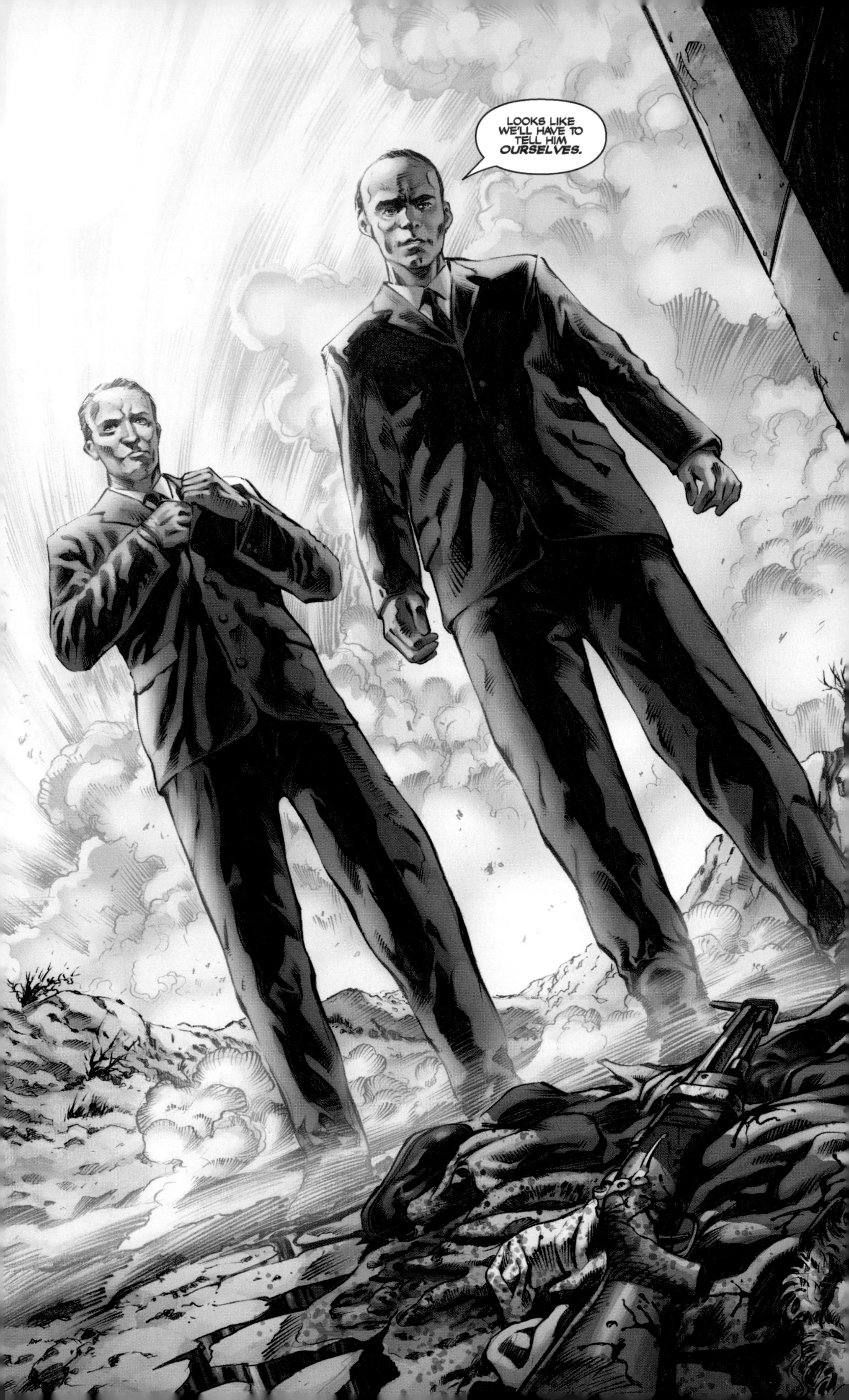
LOOKS LIKE WE'LL HAVE TO TELL HIM *OURSELVES.*

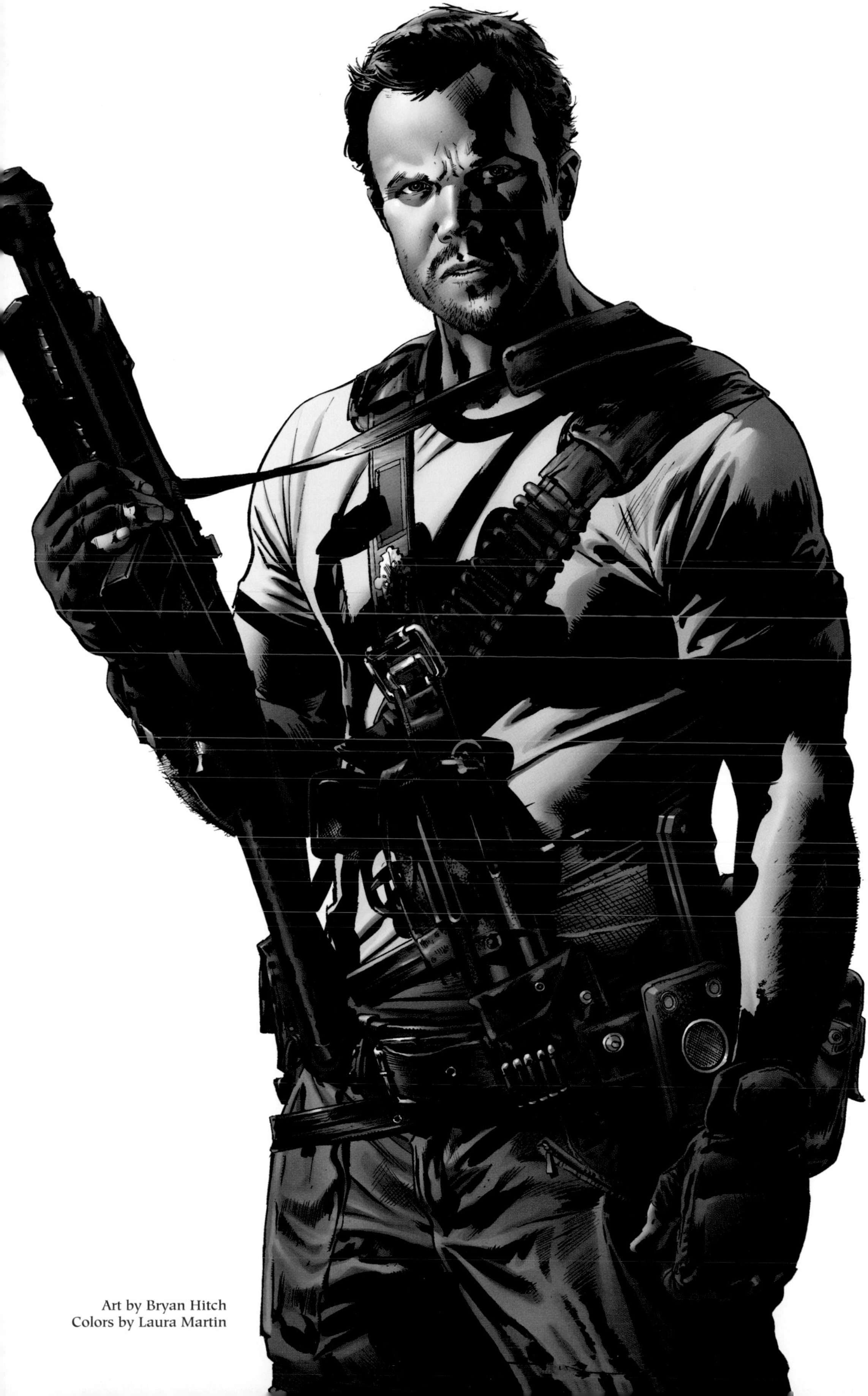

Art by Bryan Hitch
Colors by Laura Martin

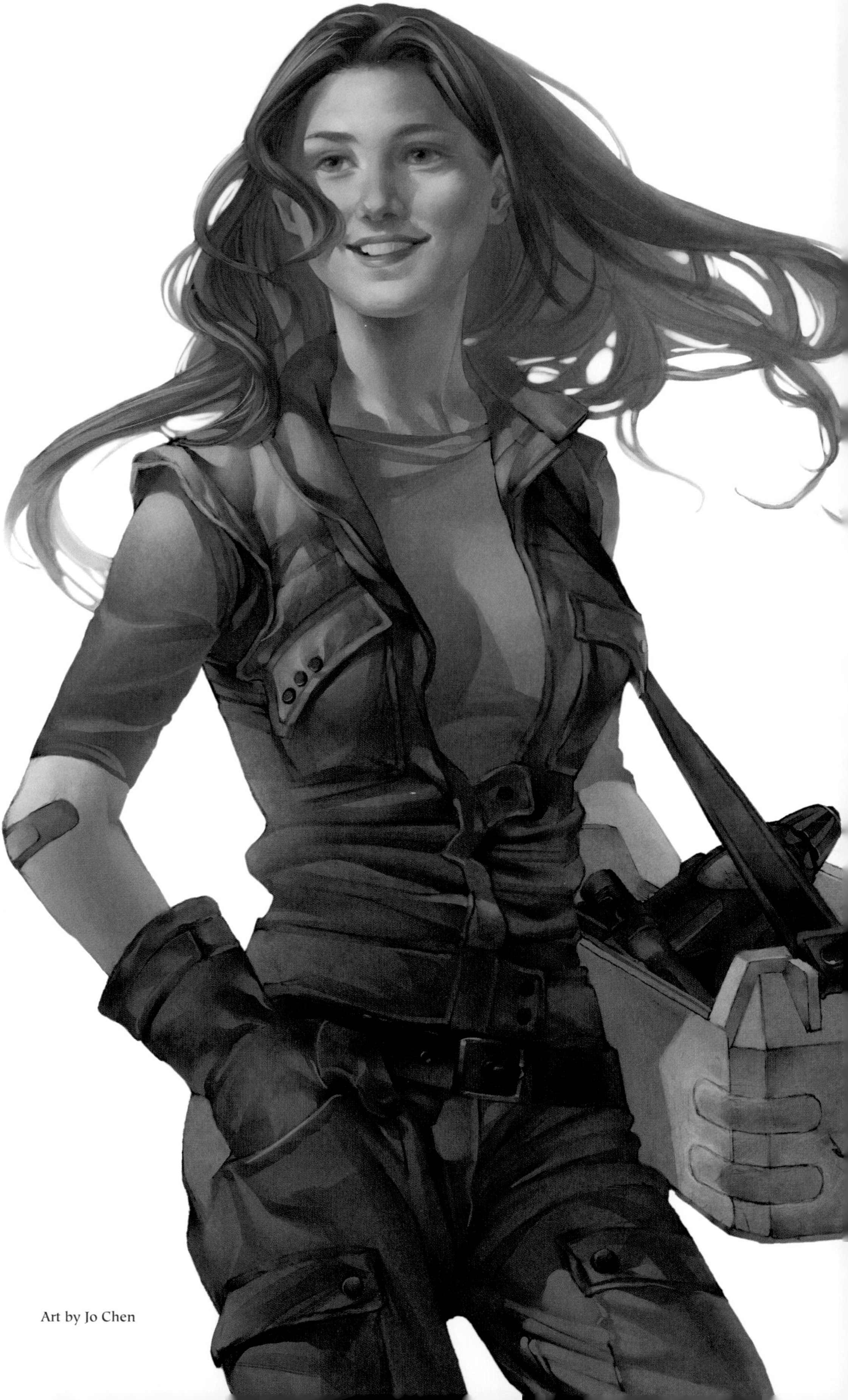

Art by Jo Chen

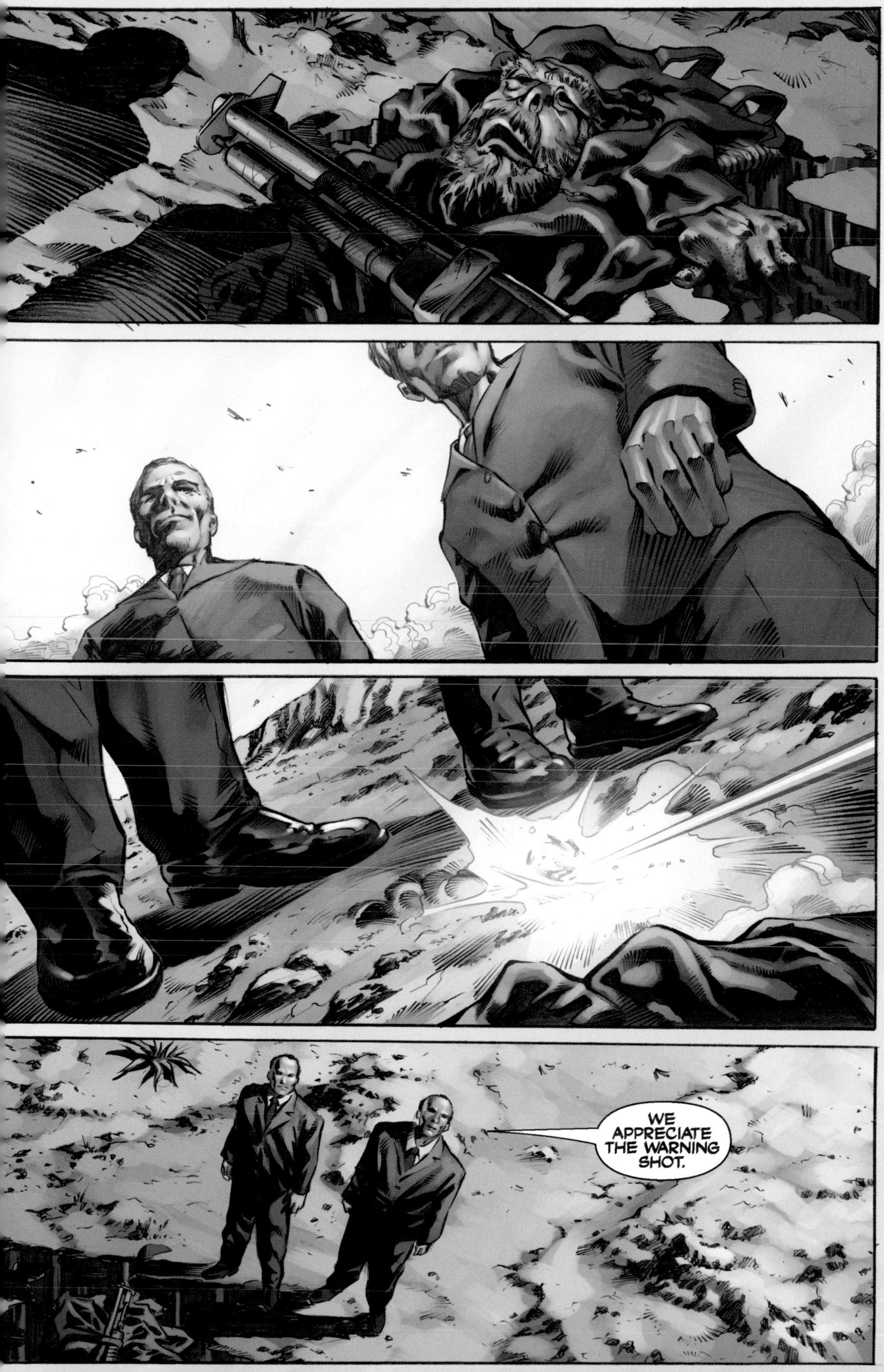
WE APPRECIATE THE WARNING SHOT.

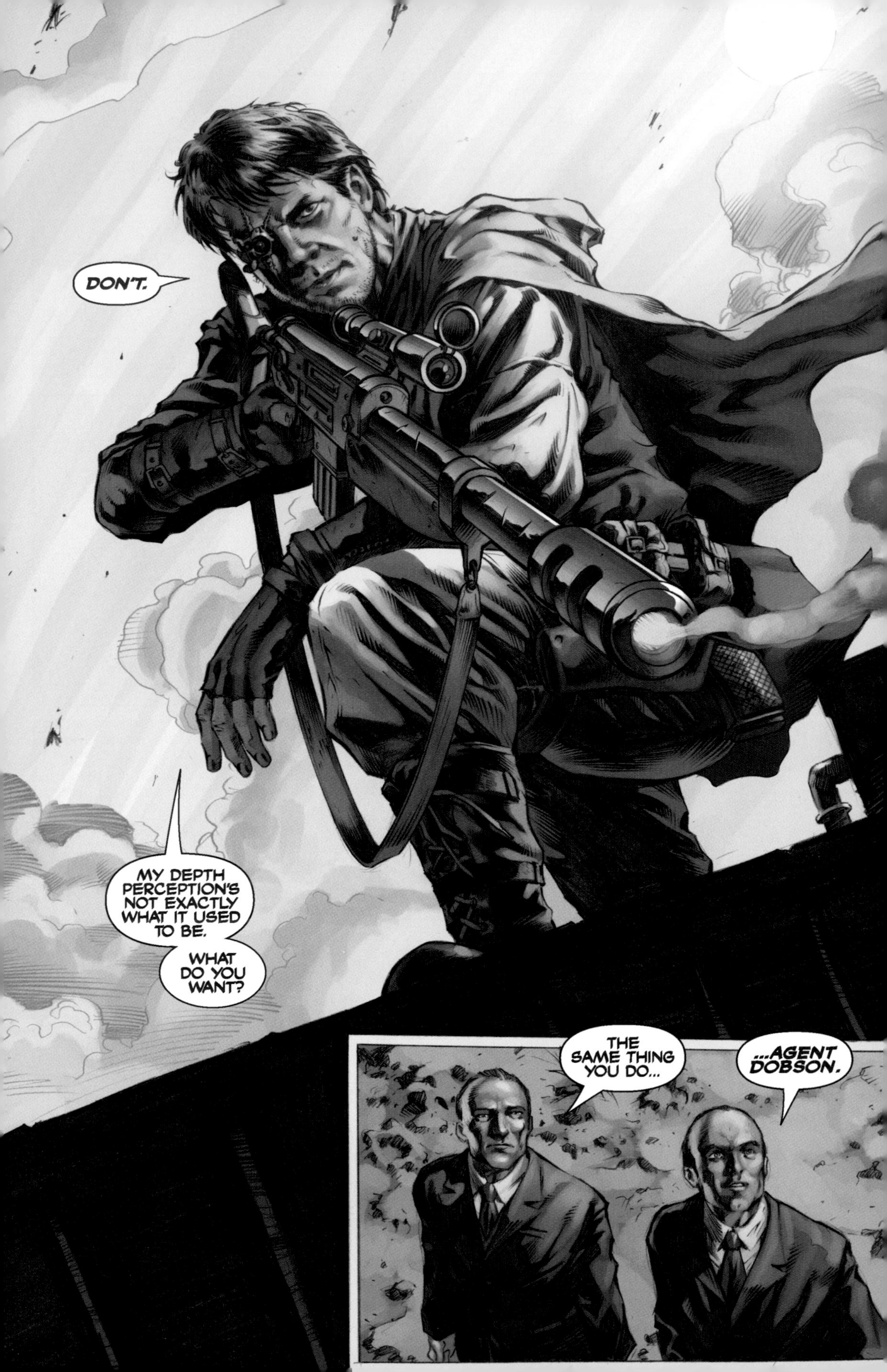
DON'T.
MY DEPTH PERCEPTION'S NOT EXACTLY WHAT IT USED TO BE.
WHAT DO YOU WANT?
THE SAME THING YOU DO...
...AGENT DOBSON.

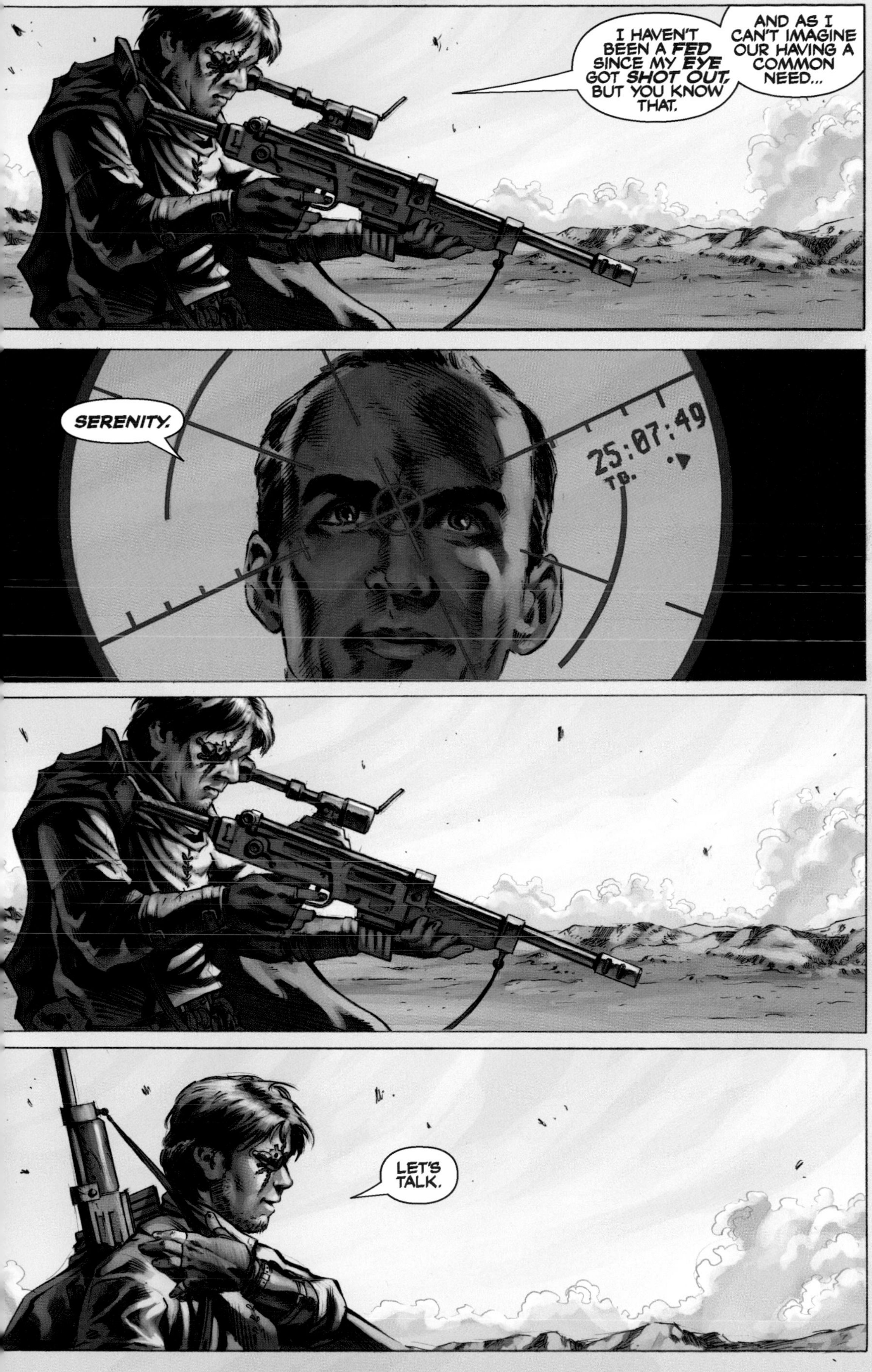
I HAVEN'T BEEN A FED SINCE MY EYE GOT SHOT OUT, BUT YOU KNOW THAT.
AND AS I CAN'T IMAGINE OUR HAVING A COMMON NEED...
SERENITY.
25:07:49
TD.
LET'S TALK.

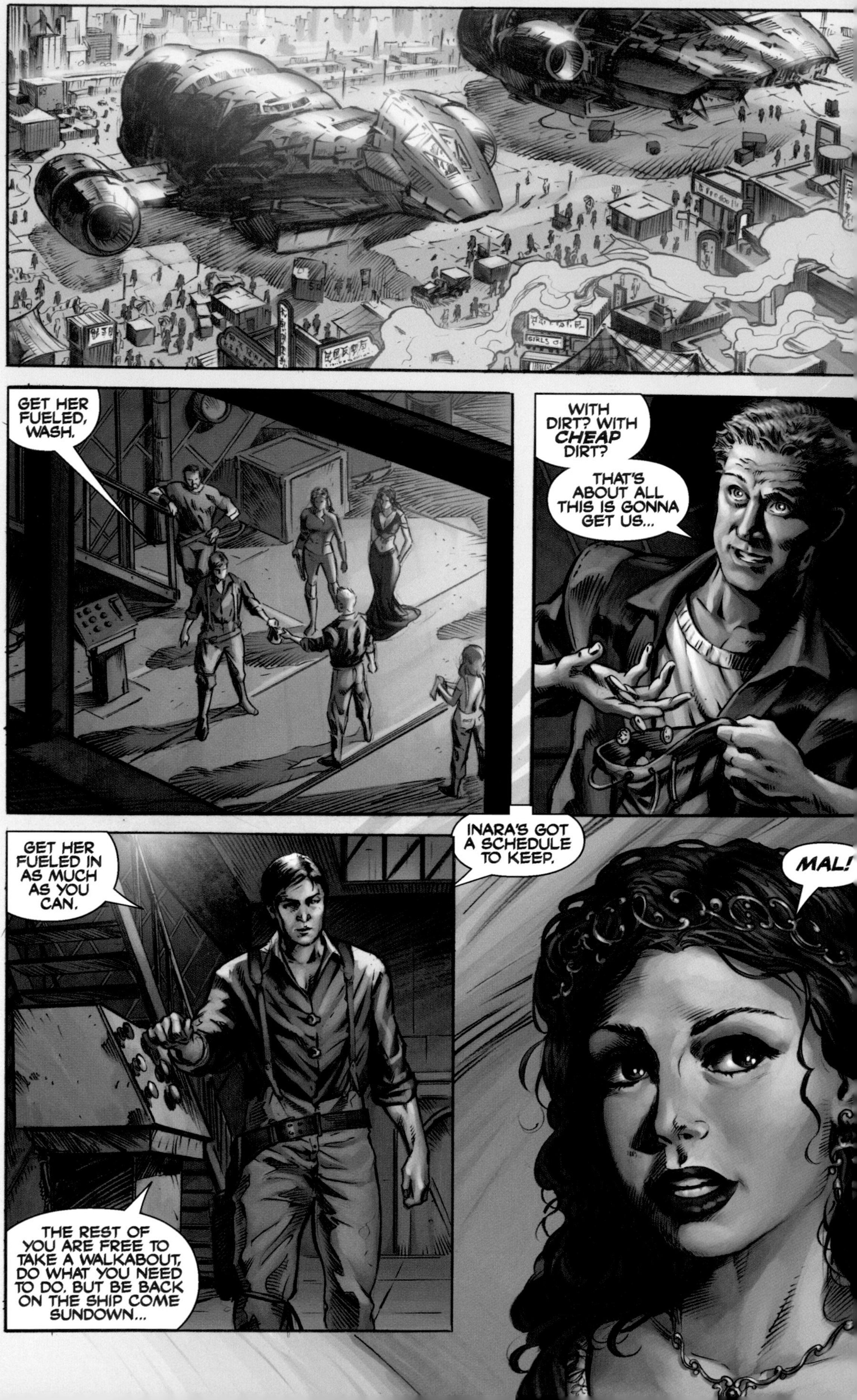
GET HER FUELED, WASH.
WITH DIRT? WITH *CHEAP* DIRT?
THAT'S ABOUT ALL THIS IS GONNA GET US...
GET HER FUELED IN AS MUCH AS YOU CAN.
INARA'S GOT A SCHEDULE TO KEEP.
THE REST OF YOU ARE FREE TO TAKE A WALKABOUT, DO WHAT YOU NEED TO DO, BUT BE BACK ON THE SHIP COME SUNDOWN...
MAL!

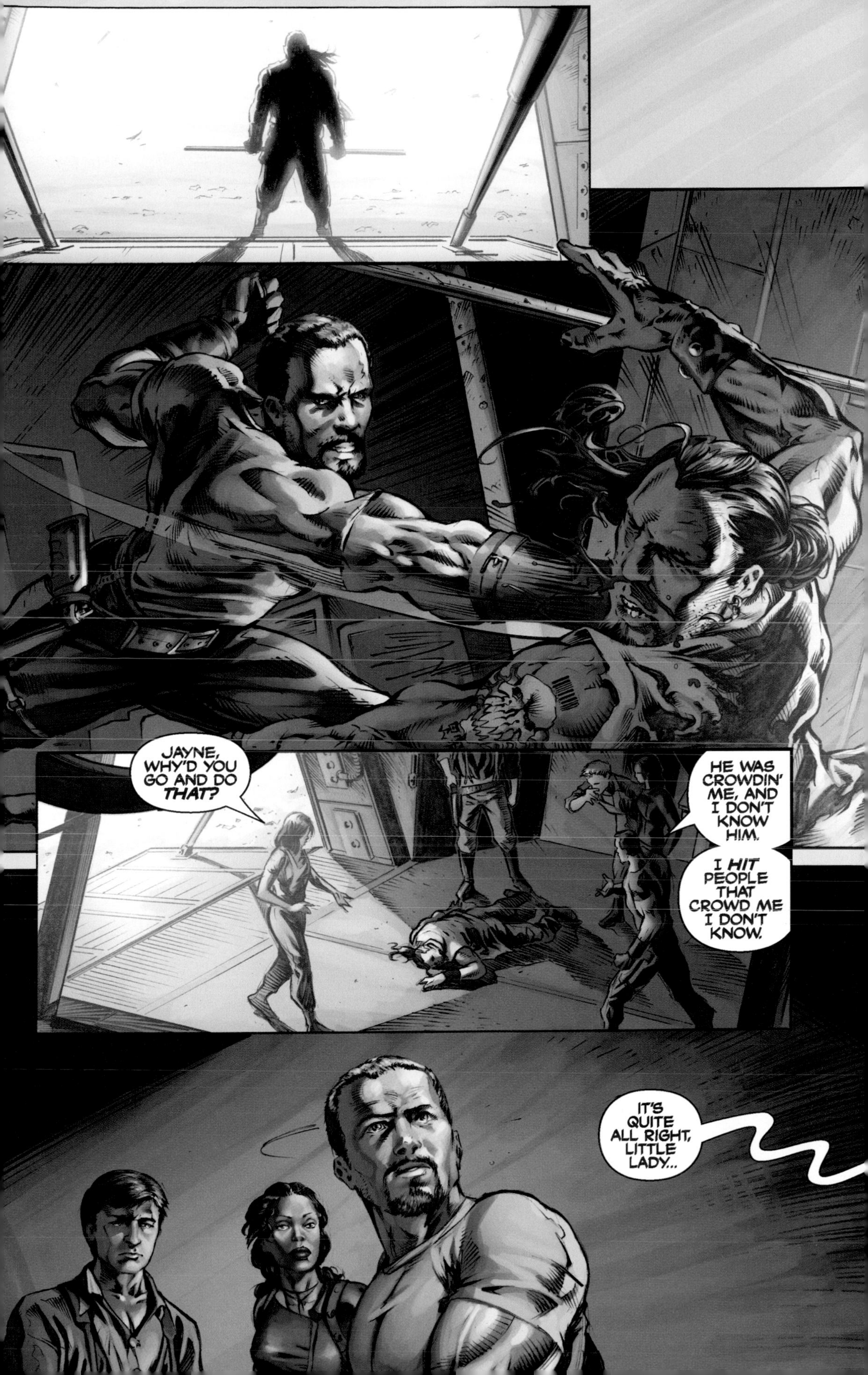
JAYNE, WHY'D YOU GO AND DO *THAT*?
HE WAS CROWDIN' ME, AND I DON'T KNOW HIM.
I *HIT* PEOPLE THAT CROWD ME I DON'T KNOW.
IT'S QUITE ALL RIGHT, LITTLE LADY...

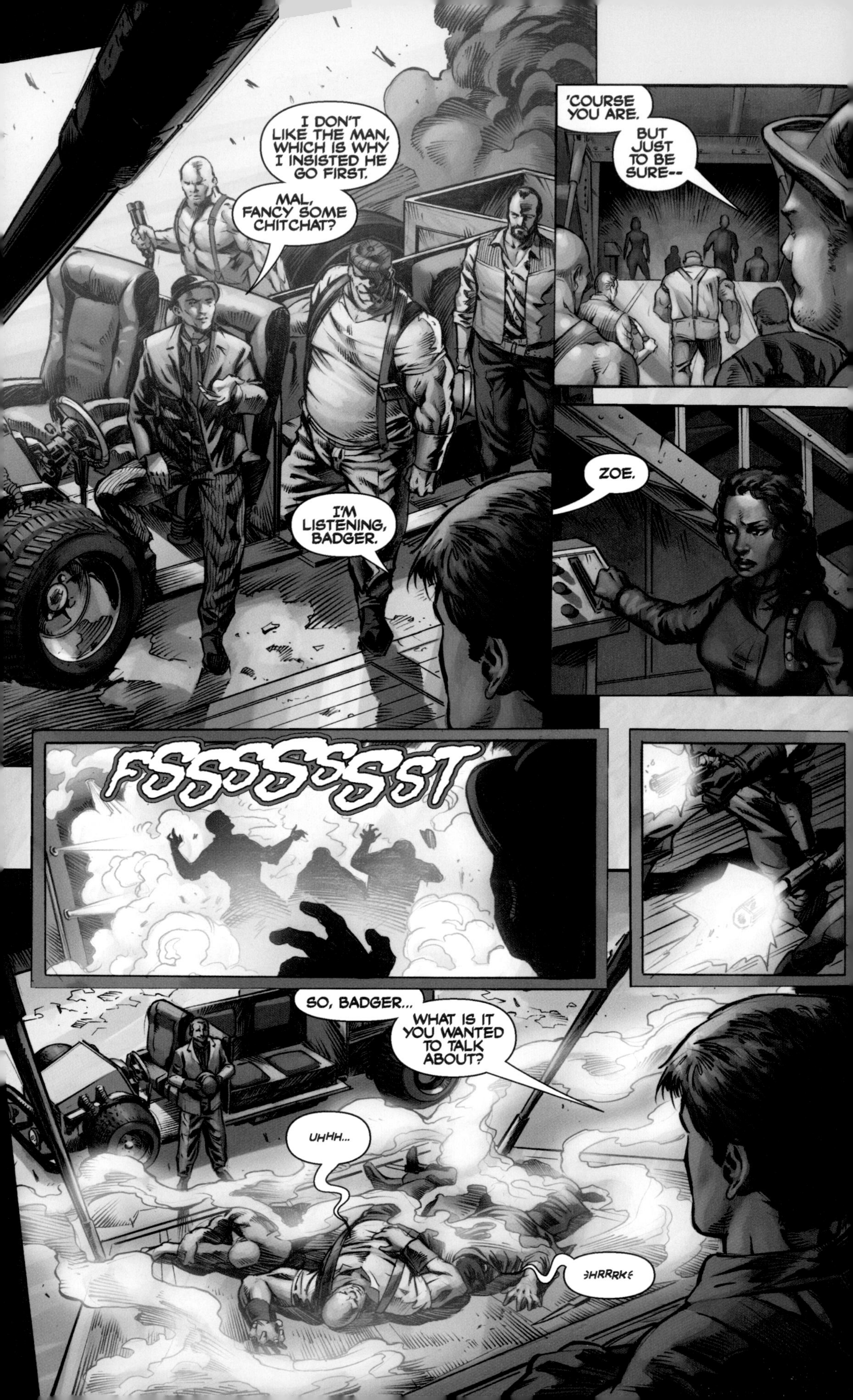
I DON'T LIKE THE MAN, WHICH IS WHY I INSISTED HE GO FIRST.
MAL, FANCY SOME CHITCHAT?
I'M LISTENING, BADGER.
'COURSE YOU ARE.
BUT JUST TO BE SURE--
ZOE.
FSSSSSSST
SO, BADGER...
WHAT IS IT YOU WANTED TO TALK ABOUT?
UHHH...
HRRRK

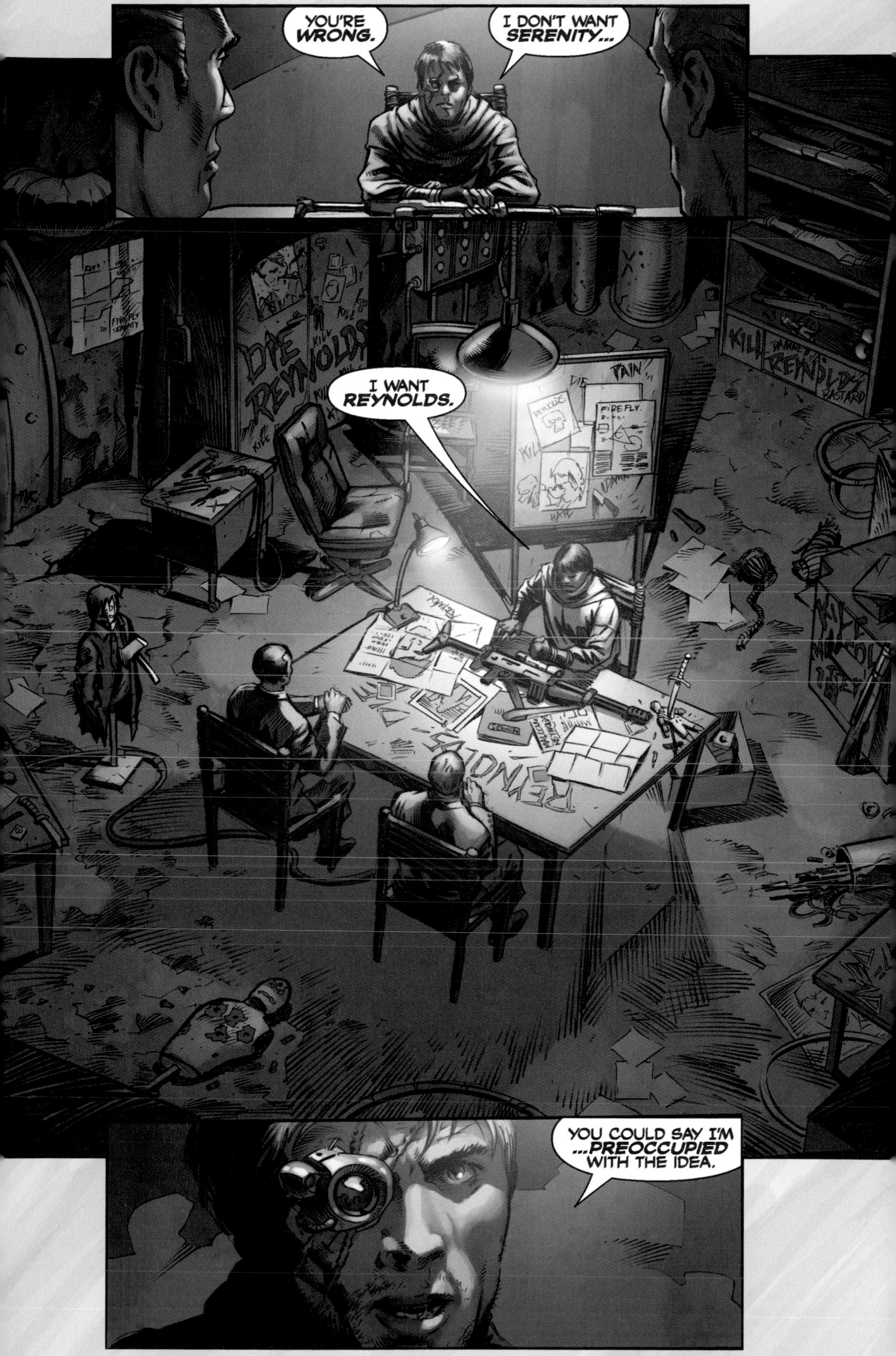
YOU'RE WRONG.
I DON'T WANT SERENITY...
I WANT REYNOLDS.
YOU COULD SAY I'M ...PREOCCUPIED WITH THE IDEA.

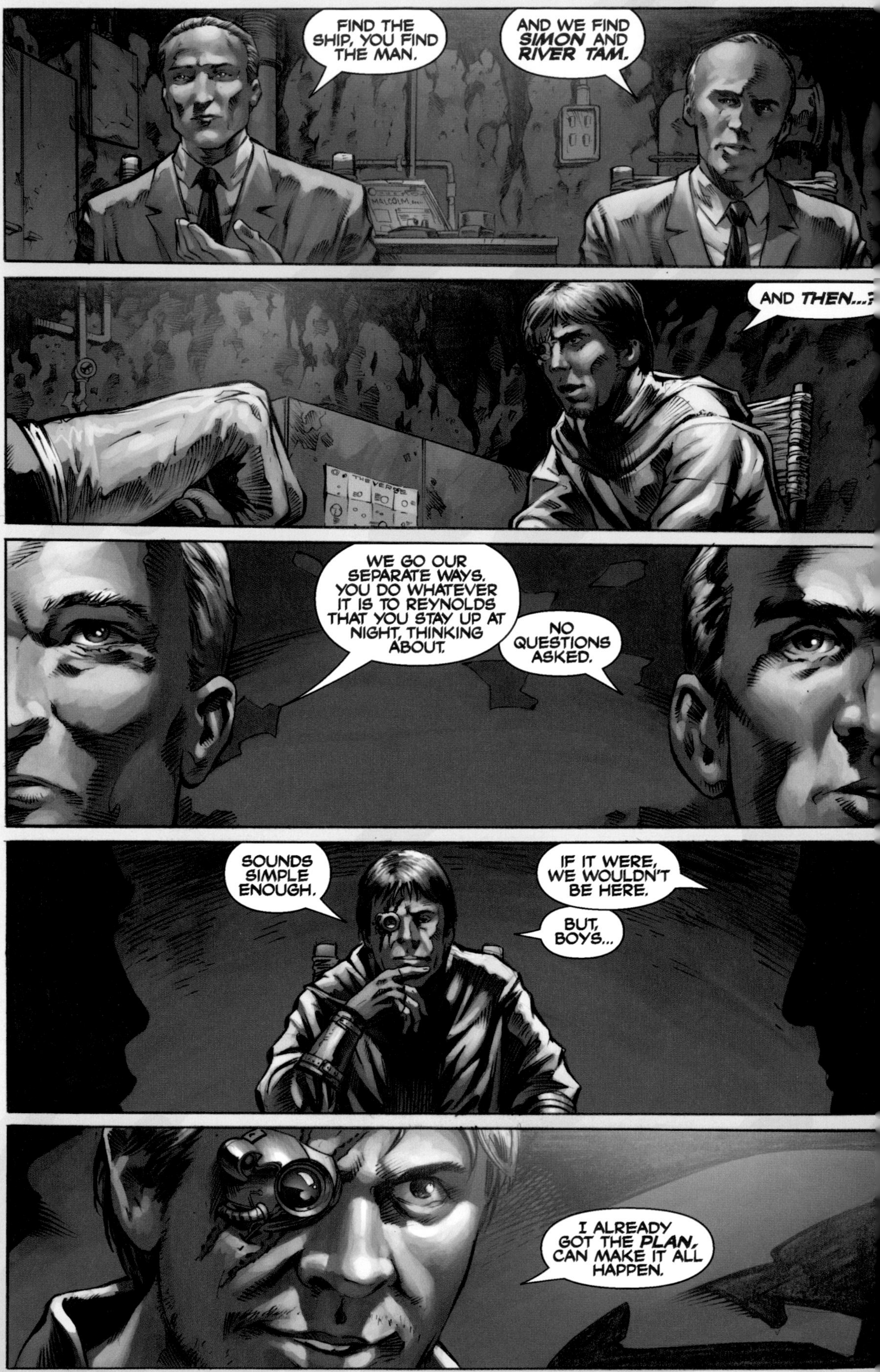
FIND THE SHIP, YOU FIND THE MAN.
AND WE FIND *SIMON* AND *RIVER TAM.*
MALCOLM...
AND *THEN*...?
THE VERSE
WE GO OUR SEPARATE WAYS. YOU DO WHATEVER IT IS TO REYNOLDS THAT YOU STAY UP AT NIGHT, THINKING ABOUT.
NO QUESTIONS ASKED.
SOUNDS SIMPLE ENOUGH.
IF IT WERE, WE WOULDN'T BE HERE.
BUT, BOYS...
I ALREADY GOT THE *PLAN*, CAN MAKE IT ALL HAPPEN.

FOR SOMEONE WHO CAME HERE TO TALK, BADGER...

YOU SURE AIN'T.

WHERE ARE YOU TAKING ME?

THAT'S NOT YOUR CONCERN, NOW SPILL YOUR GUTS...

OR I MIGHT LET JAYNE.

OH, YEAH.

CAPTAIN, SHOULD WE BE *WANTING* TO HEAR THE LIKES OF HIM OUT?

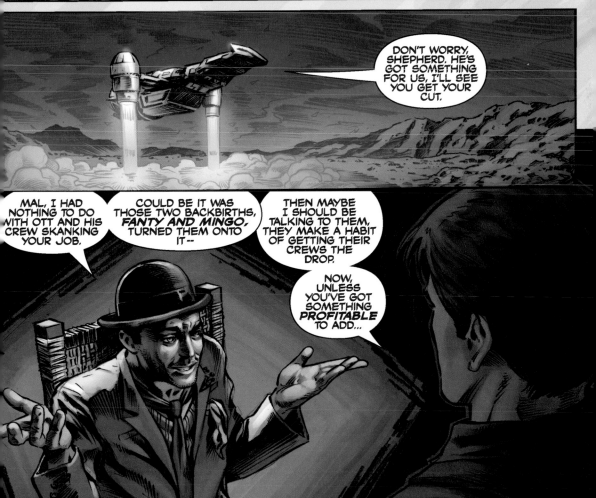

DON'T WORRY, SHEPHERD. HE'S GOT SOMETHING FOR US, I'LL SEE YOU GET YOUR CUT.

MAL, I HAD NOTHING TO DO WITH OTT AND HIS CREW SKANKING YOUR JOB.

COULD BE IT WAS THOSE TWO BACKBIRTHS, *FANTY AND MINGO,* TURNED THEM ONTO IT--

THEN MAYBE I SHOULD BE TALKING TO THEM, THEY MAKE A HABIT OF GETTING THEIR CREWS THE DROP.

NOW, UNLESS YOU'VE GOT SOMETHING *PROFITABLE* TO ADD...

THE BATTLE OF STURGES.

HEARD OF IT?

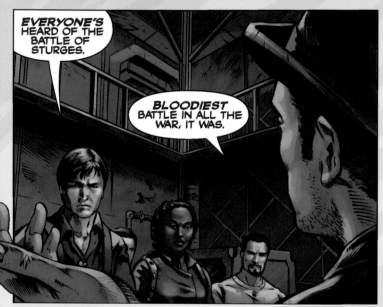

EVERYONE'S HEARD OF THE BATTLE OF STURGES.

BLOODIEST BATTLE IN ALL THE WAR, IT WAS.

I'D HOLD IT WAS A DISTANT *SECOND.*

BUT GO ON.

SHORTEST, TOO. ALL THOSE LIVES...

WANNA HEAR 'BOUT *COIN,* NOT SOME RUTTIN' HISTORY LESSON.

...SNUFFED IN A BLINK.

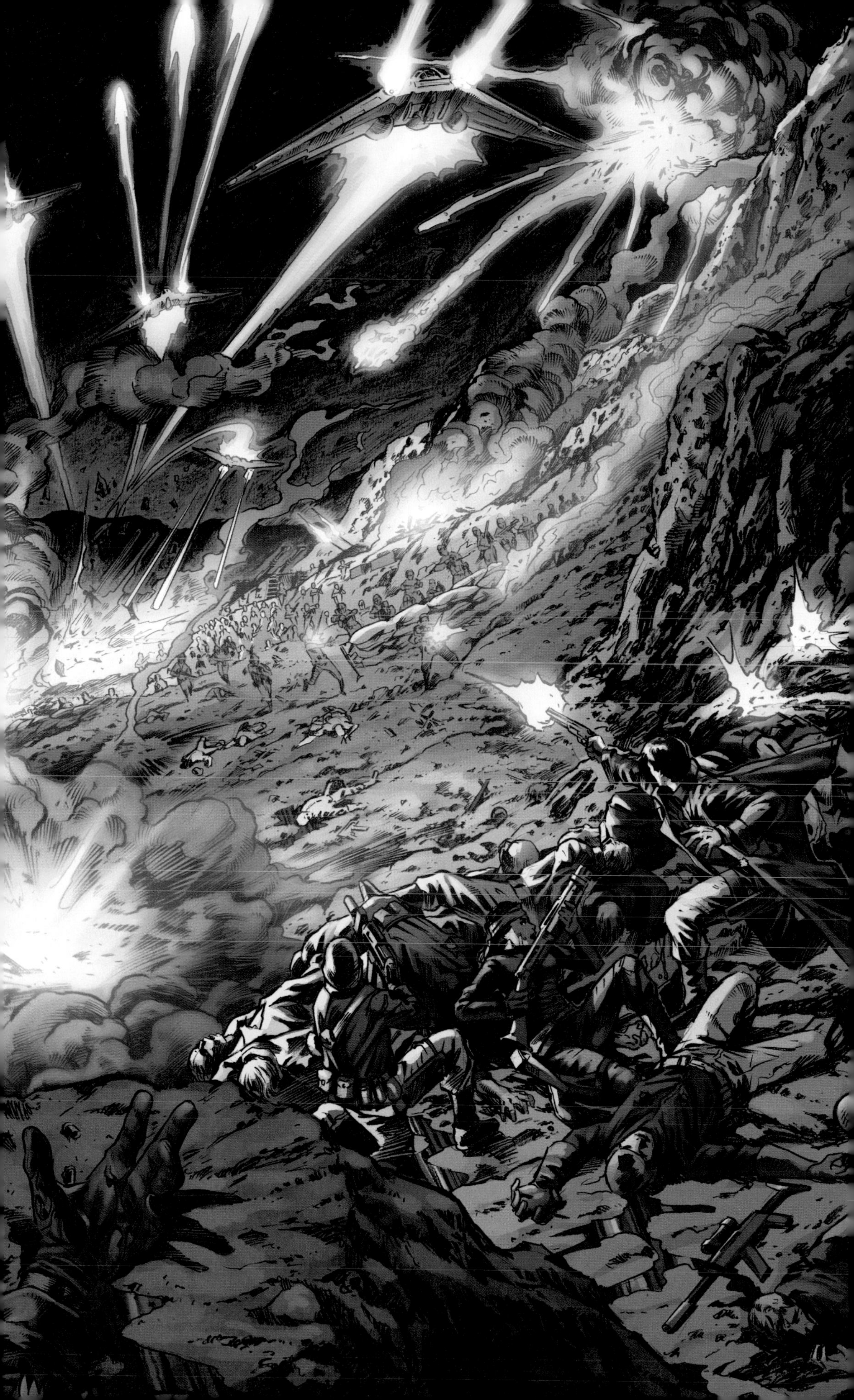

A BLINK'S AN AWFUL LONG TIME WHEN YOU'RE ON THE GROUND.

WE'RE NOT REQUIRIN' A LECTURE ON THE SUBJECT, OR HAD YOU NOT NOTICED THE *COLOR* THE CAPTAIN AND I ARE PARTIAL TO WEARING?

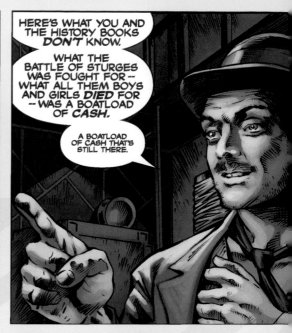

HERE'S WHAT YOU AND THE HISTORY BOOKS *DON'T* KNOW.

WHAT THE BATTLE OF STURGES WAS FOUGHT FOR -- WHAT ALL THEM BOYS AND GIRLS *DIED* FOR -- WAS A BOATLOAD OF *CASH*.

A BOATLOAD OF CASH THAT'S STILL THERE.

THE *COORDINATES*, MAL.

TAKE YOU RIGHT TO THE BATTLEFIELD -- AND THE STASH OF *REAL* THEM *BROWNCOATS* GOT BUTCHERED OVER. IT'S JUST SITTING THERE FOR YOU, OR SOMEONE NEAR ENOUGH YOU, TO SNATCH IT UP.

LESS MY *PERCENTAGE*, OF COURSE.

WHAT DO YOU SAY?

I SAY I'LL THINK ABOUT IT.

NOW GET OFF MY SHIP BEFORE THE STAIN SETS.

"YOU'VE GOT A LONG WALK AHEAD OF YOU."

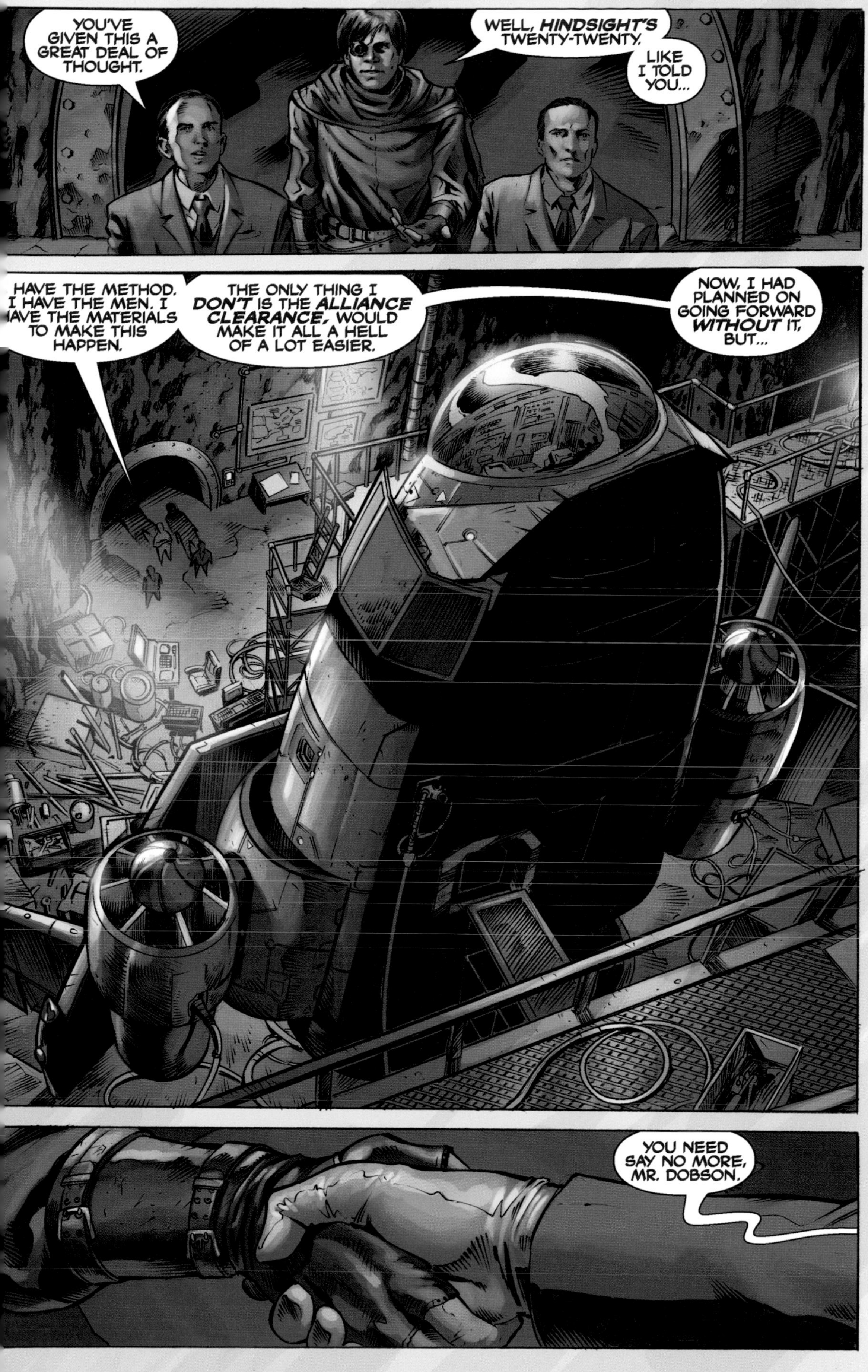
YOU'VE GIVEN THIS A GREAT DEAL OF THOUGHT.
WELL, ***HINDSIGHT'S*** TWENTY-TWENTY.
LIKE I TOLD YOU...
HAVE THE METHOD. I HAVE THE MEN. I AVE THE MATERIALS TO MAKE THIS HAPPEN.
THE ONLY THING I ***DON'T*** IS THE ***ALLIANCE CLEARANCE,*** WOULD MAKE IT ALL A HELL OF A LOT EASIER.
NOW, I HAD PLANNED ON GOING FORWARD ***WITHOUT*** IT, BUT...
YOU NEED SAY NO MORE, MR. DOBSON.

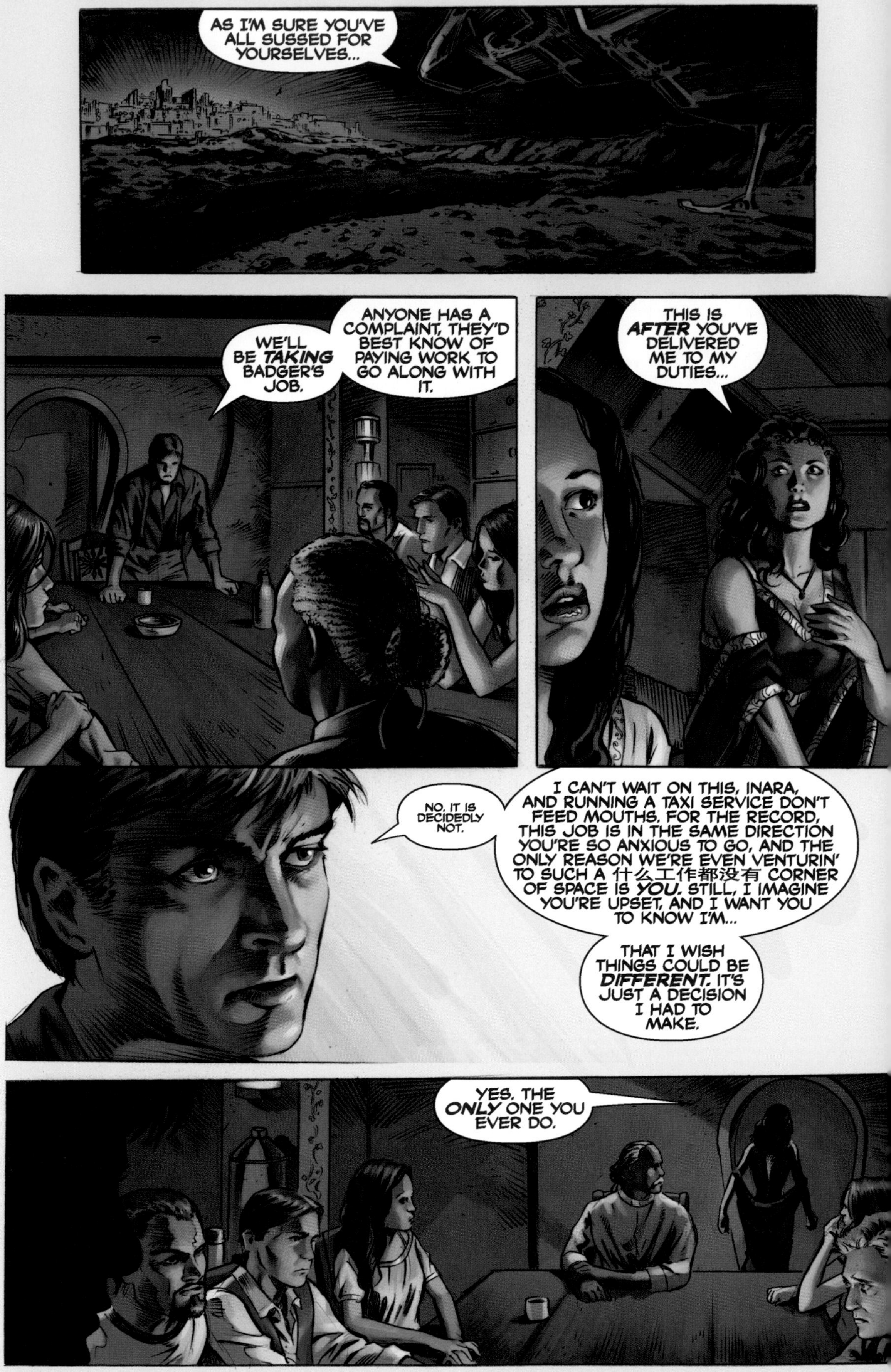
AS I'M SURE YOU'VE ALL SUSSED FOR YOURSELVES...
WE'LL BE TAKING BADGER'S JOB.
ANYONE HAS A COMPLAINT, THEY'D BEST KNOW OF PAYING WORK TO GO ALONG WITH IT.
THIS IS AFTER YOU'VE DELIVERED ME TO MY DUTIES...
NO, IT IS DECIDEDLY NOT.
I CAN'T WAIT ON THIS, INARA, AND RUNNING A TAXI SERVICE DON'T FEED MOUTHS. FOR THE RECORD, THIS JOB IS IN THE SAME DIRECTION YOU'RE SO ANXIOUS TO GO, AND THE ONLY REASON WE'RE EVEN VENTURIN' TO SUCH A 什么工作都没有 CORNER OF SPACE IS YOU. STILL, I IMAGINE YOU'RE UPSET, AND I WANT YOU TO KNOW I'M...
THAT I WISH THINGS COULD BE DIFFERENT. IT'S JUST A DECISION I HAD TO MAKE.
YES. THE ONLY ONE YOU EVER DO.

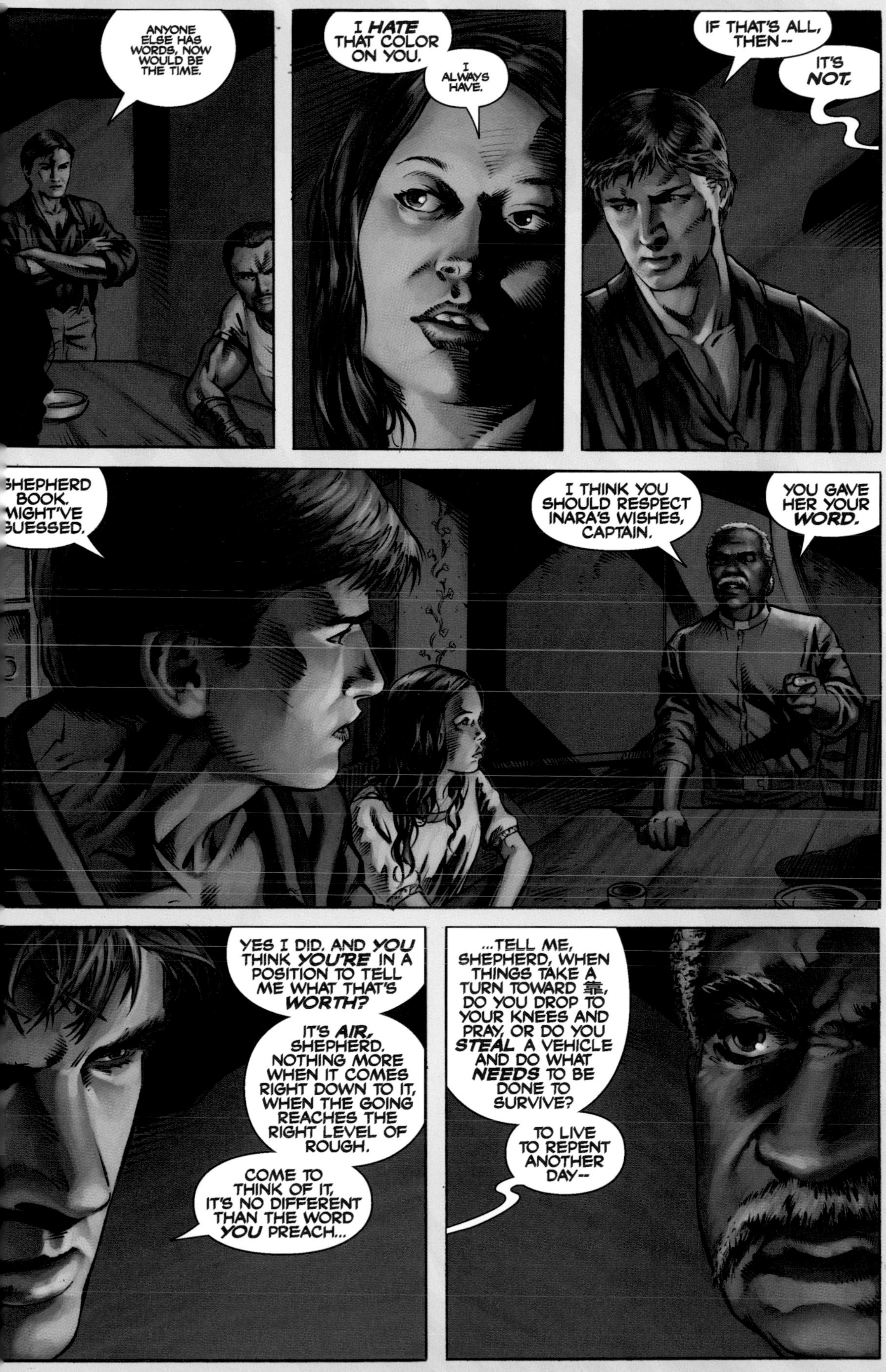
ANYONE ELSE HAS WORDS, NOW WOULD BE THE TIME.
I HATE THAT COLOR ON YOU.
I ALWAYS HAVE.
IF THAT'S ALL, THEN--
IT'S NOT.
SHEPHERD BOOK. MIGHT'VE GUESSED.
I THINK YOU SHOULD RESPECT INARA'S WISHES, CAPTAIN.
YOU GAVE HER YOUR WORD.
YES I DID. AND YOU THINK YOU'RE IN A POSITION TO TELL ME WHAT THAT'S WORTH?
IT'S AIR, SHEPHERD. NOTHING MORE WHEN IT COMES RIGHT DOWN TO IT, WHEN THE GOING REACHES THE RIGHT LEVEL OF ROUGH.
COME TO THINK OF IT, IT'S NO DIFFERENT THAN THE WORD YOU PREACH...
...TELL ME, SHEPHERD, WHEN THINGS TAKE A TURN TOWARD 靠, DO YOU DROP TO YOUR KNEES AND PRAY, OR DO YOU STEAL A VEHICLE AND DO WHAT NEEDS TO BE DONE TO SURVIVE?
TO LIVE TO REPENT ANOTHER DAY--

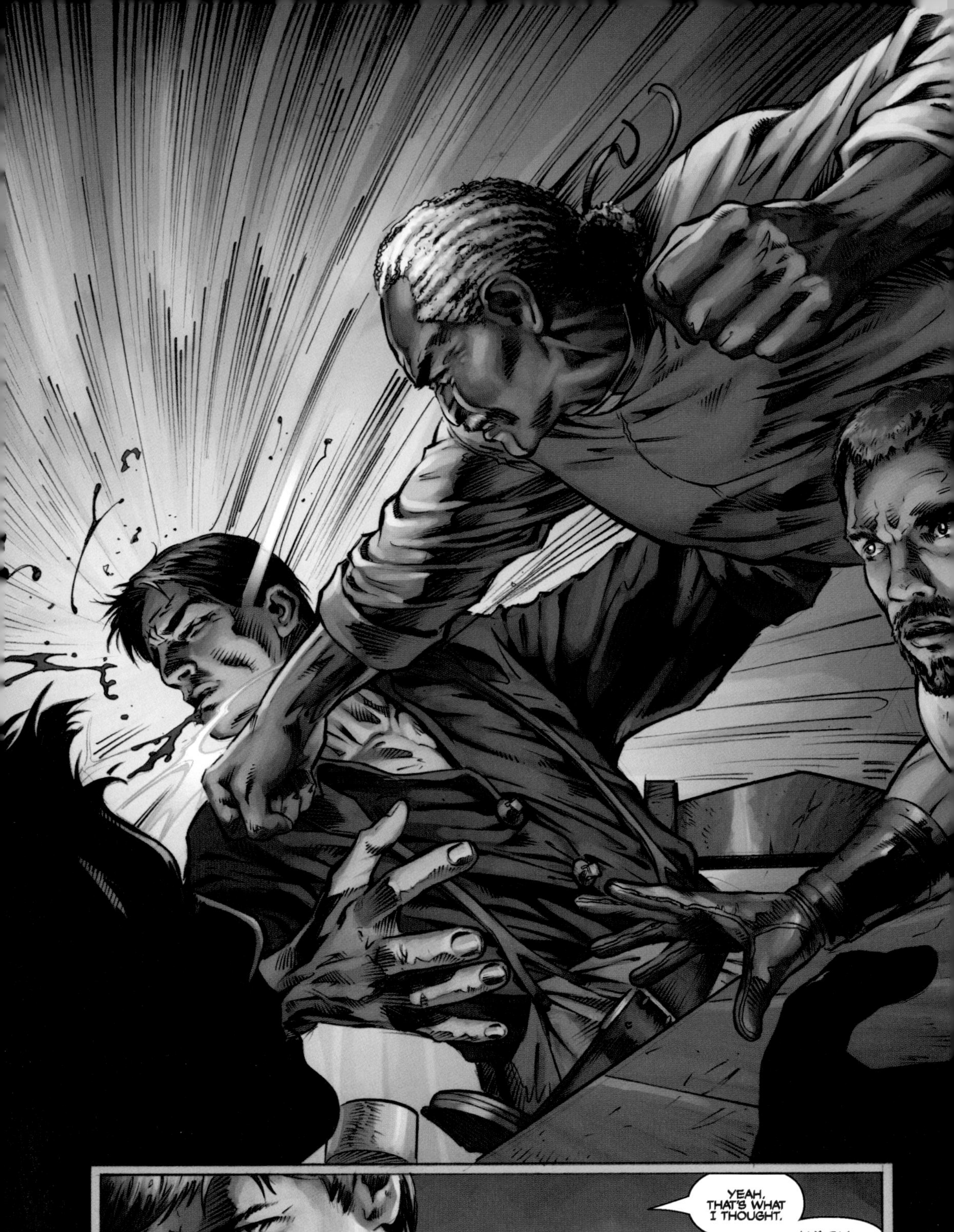

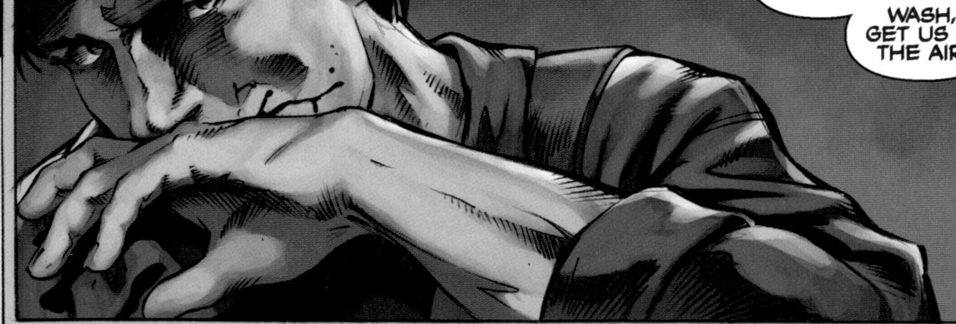
YEAH, THAT'S WHAT I THOUGHT.
WASH, GET US IN THE AIR.

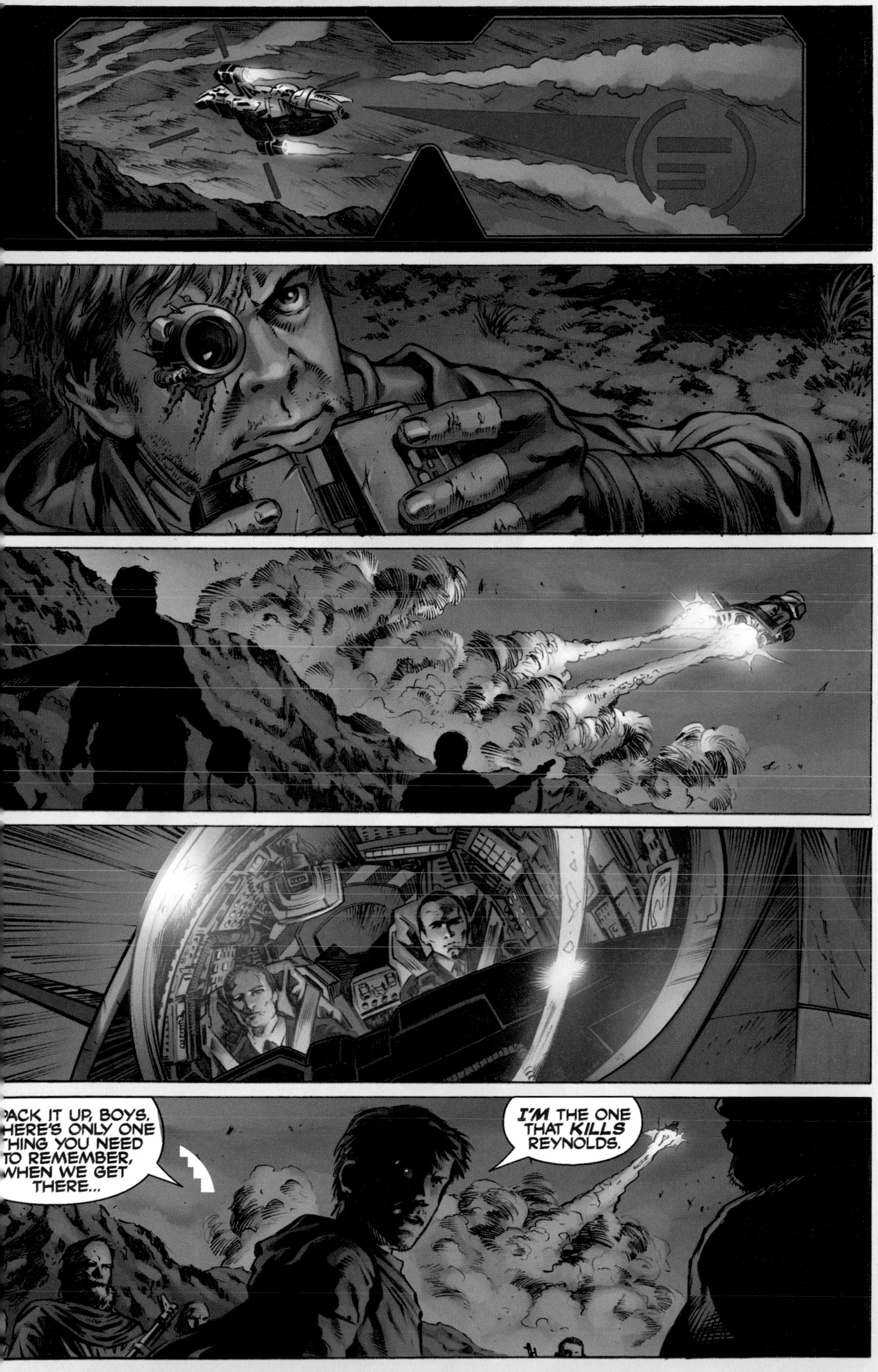
PACK IT UP, BOYS. HERE'S ONLY ONE THING YOU NEED TO REMEMBER, WHEN WE GET THERE...
I'M THE ONE THAT KILLS REYNOLDS.

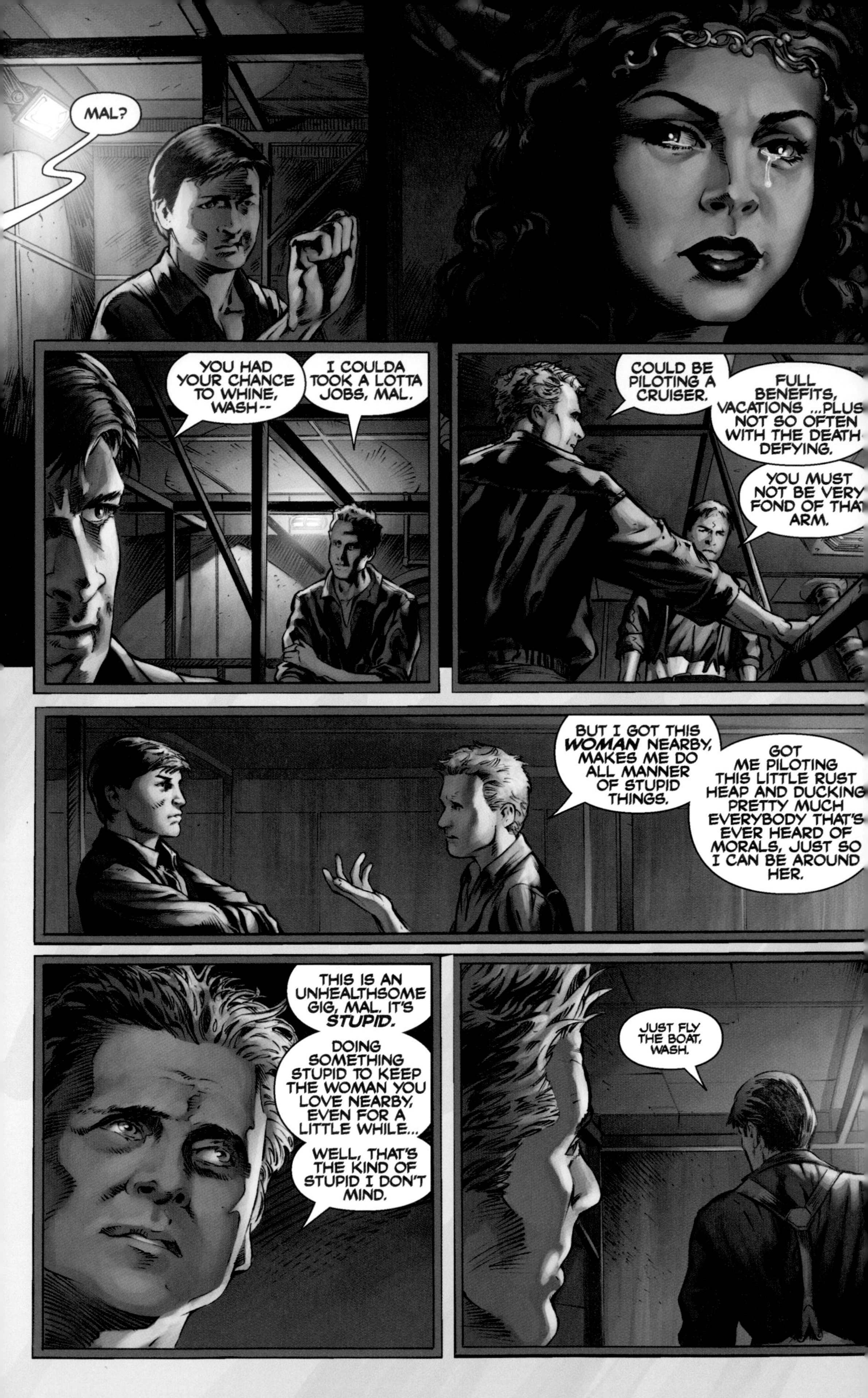
MAL?
YOU HAD YOUR CHANCE TO WHINE, WASH--
I COULDA TOOK A LOTTA JOBS, MAL.
COULD BE PILOTING A CRUISER.
FULL BENEFITS, VACATIONS ...PLUS NOT SO OFTEN WITH THE DEATH DEFYING.
YOU MUST NOT BE VERY FOND OF THAT ARM.
BUT I GOT THIS WOMAN NEARBY, MAKES ME DO ALL MANNER OF STUPID THINGS.
GOT ME PILOTING THIS LITTLE RUST HEAP AND DUCKING PRETTY MUCH EVERYBODY THAT'S EVER HEARD OF MORALS, JUST SO I CAN BE AROUND HER.
THIS IS AN UNHEALTHSOME GIG, MAL. IT'S STUPID.
DOING SOMETHING STUPID TO KEEP THE WOMAN YOU LOVE NEARBY, EVEN FOR A LITTLE WHILE...
WELL, THAT'S THE KIND OF STUPID I DON'T MIND.
JUST FLY THE BOAT, WASH.

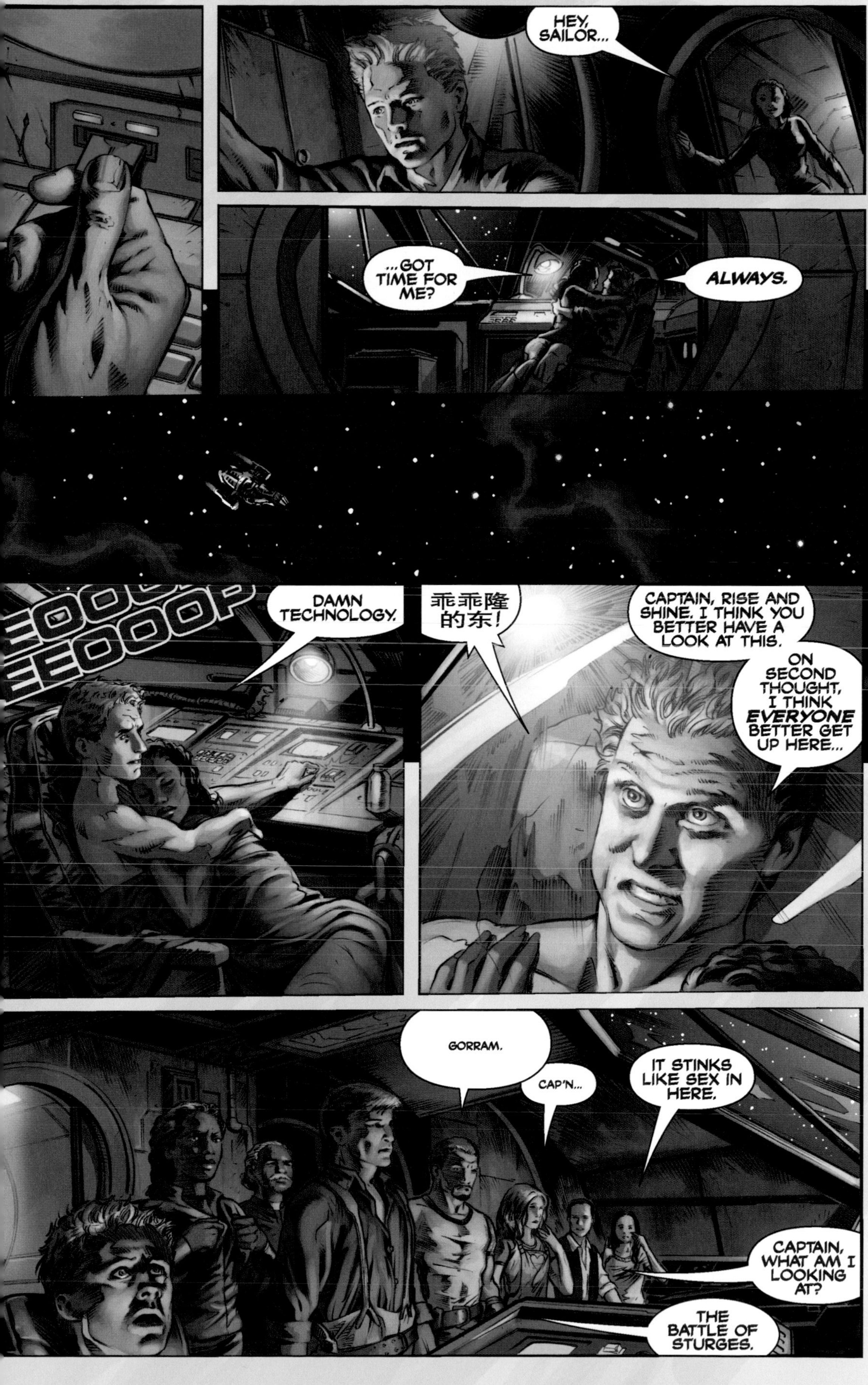
HEY, SAILOR...
...GOT TIME FOR ME?
ALWAYS.
EEOOOP
DAMN TECHNOLOGY.
乖乖隆的东!
CAPTAIN, RISE AND SHINE. I THINK YOU BETTER HAVE A LOOK AT THIS.
ON SECOND THOUGHT, I THINK EVERYONE BETTER GET UP HERE...
GORRAM.
CAP'N...
IT STINKS LIKE SEX IN HERE.
CAPTAIN, WHAT AM I LOOKING AT?
THE BATTLE OF STURGES.

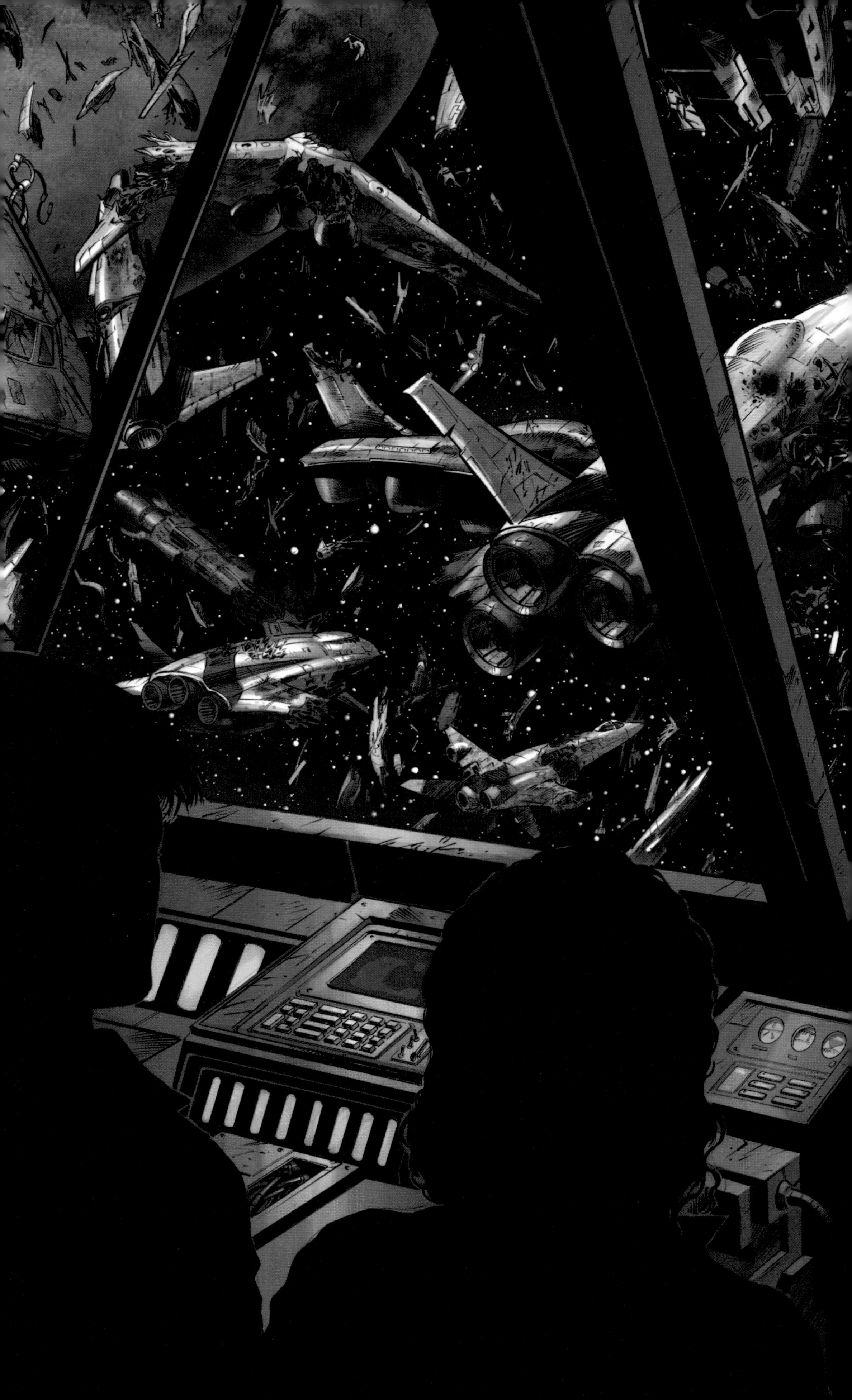

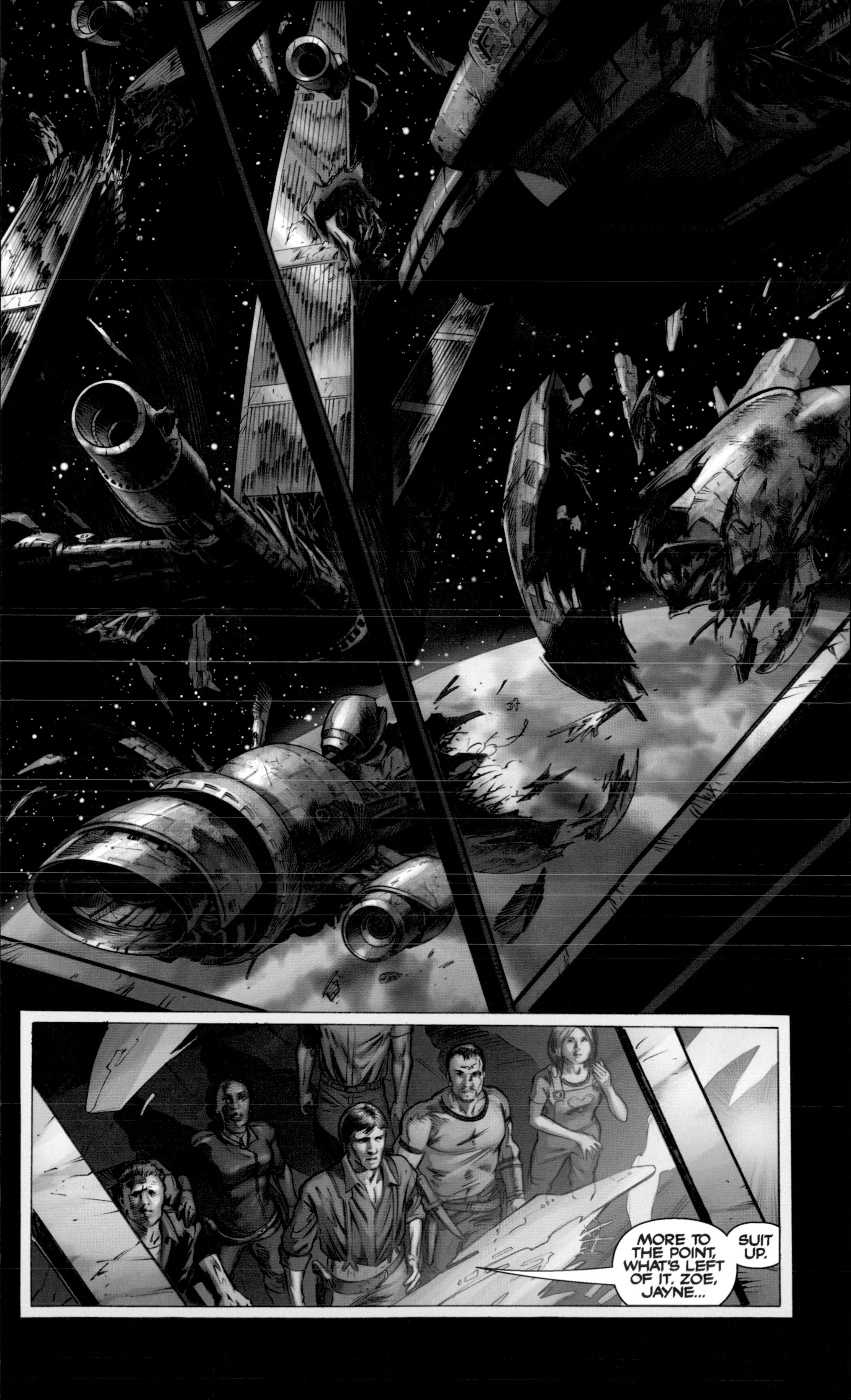
MORE TO THE POINT, WHAT'S LEFT OF IT. ZOE, JAYNE...
SUIT UP.

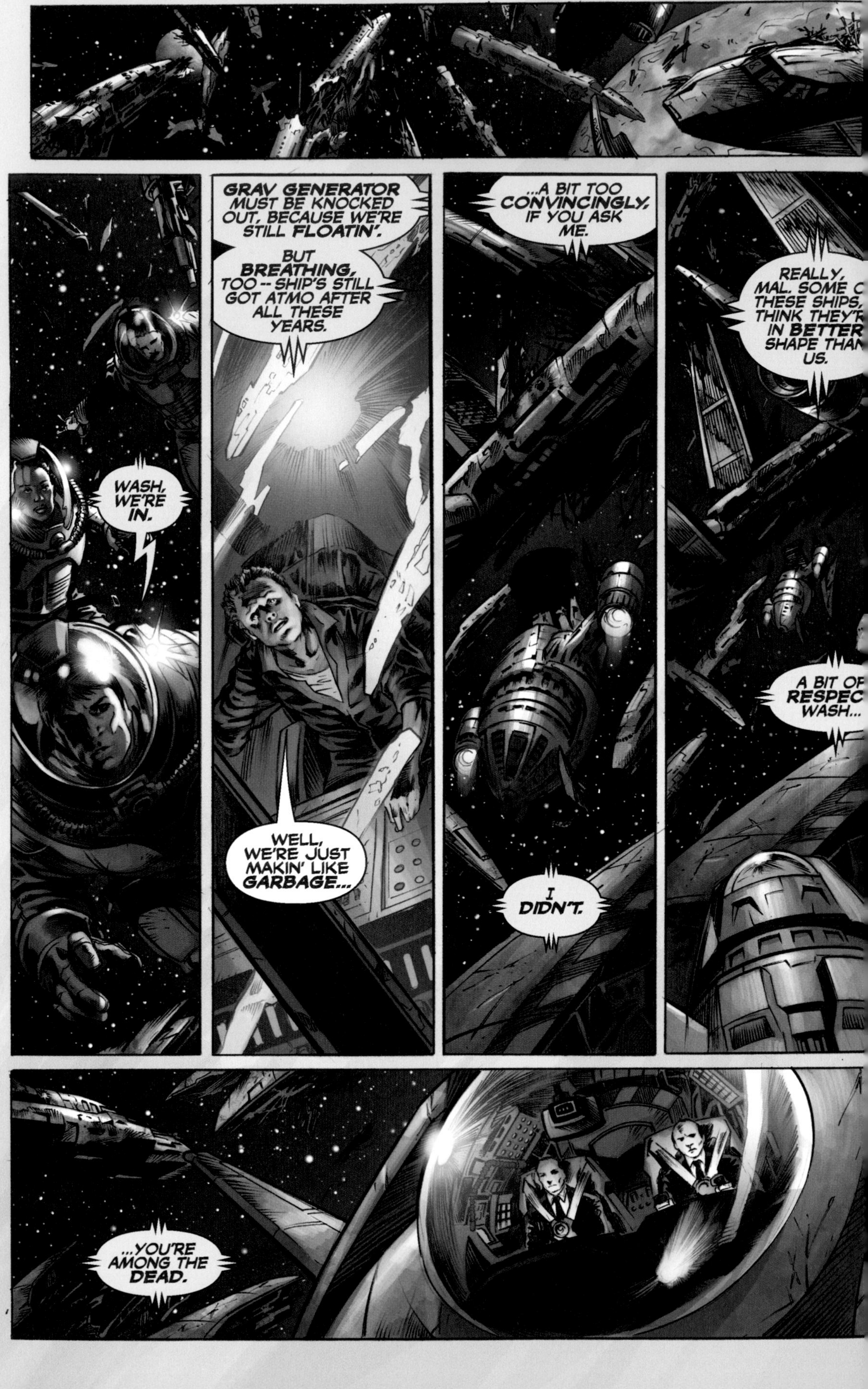
WASH, WE'RE IN.
GRAV GENERATOR MUST BE KNOCKED OUT, BECAUSE WE'RE STILL FLOATIN'.
BUT BREATHING, TOO -- SHIP'S STILL GOT ATMO AFTER ALL THESE YEARS.
WELL, WE'RE JUST MAKIN' LIKE GARBAGE...
...A BIT TOO CONVINCINGLY, IF YOU ASK ME.
I DIDN'T.
REALLY, MAL. SOME C THESE SHIPS, THINK THEY'R IN BETTER SHAPE THAN US.
A BIT OF RESPEC WASH...
...YOU'RE AMONG THE DEAD.

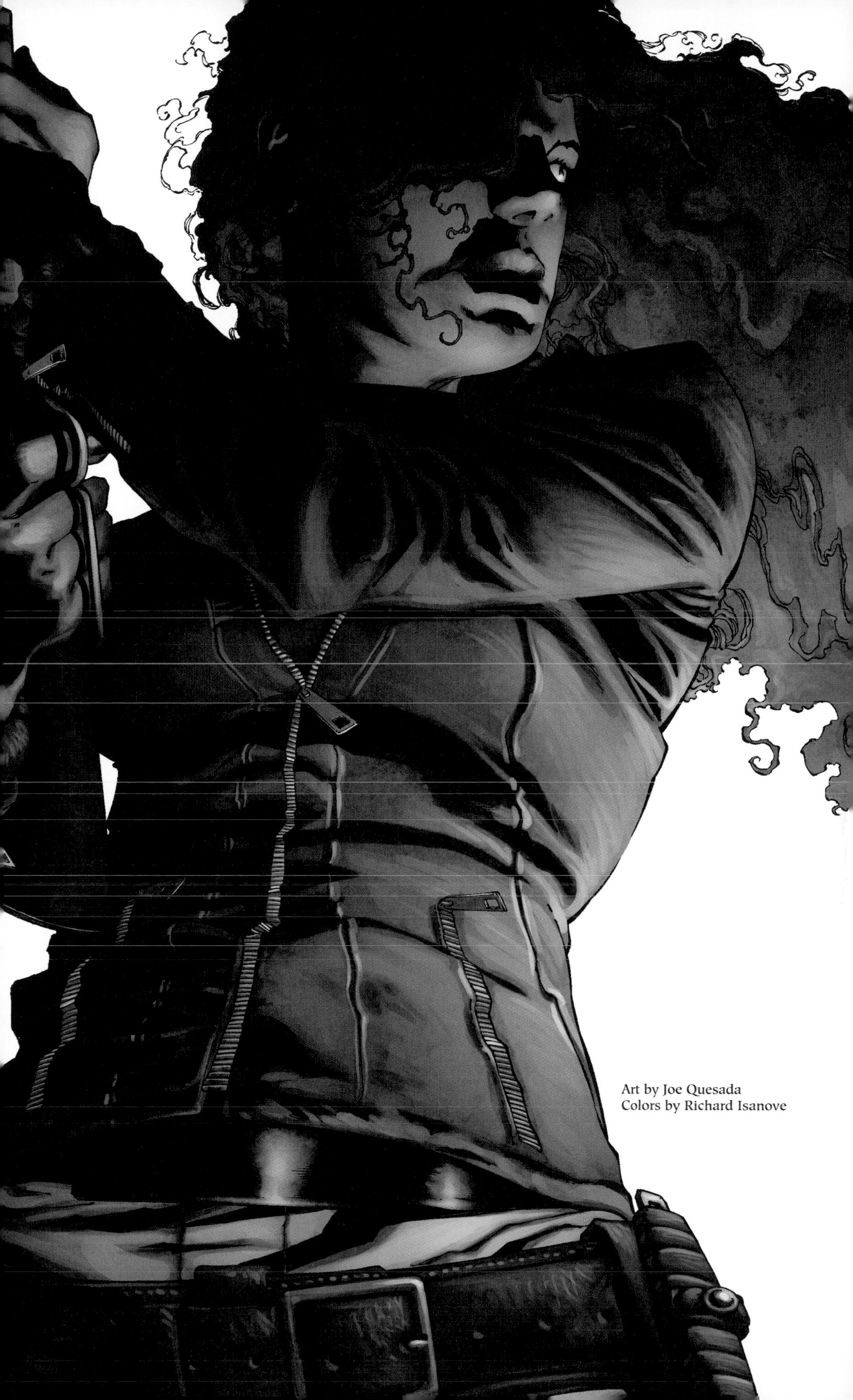

Art by Joe Quesada
Colors by Richard Isanove

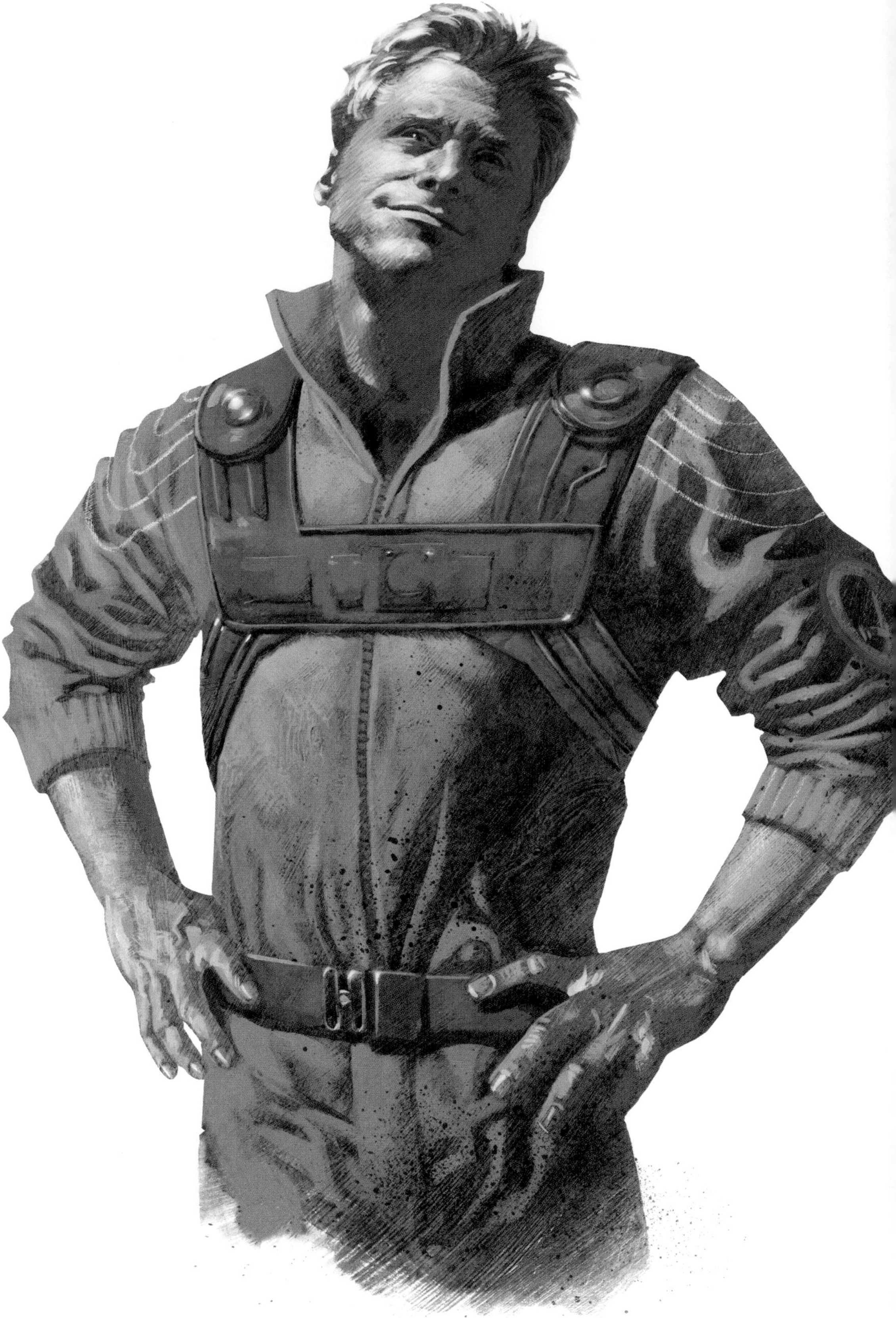

Art by Sean Phillips

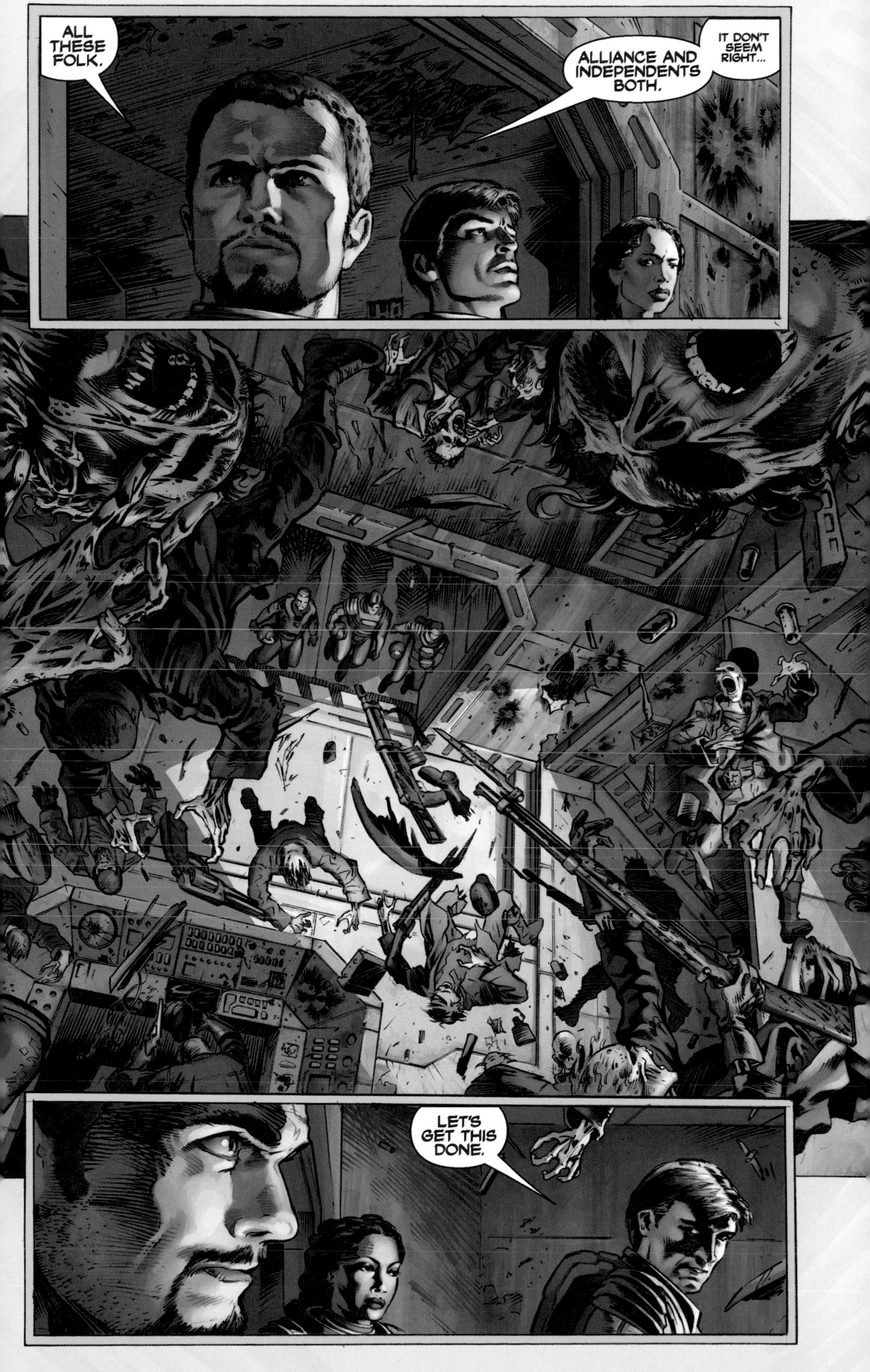
ALL THESE FOLK.
ALLIANCE AND INDEPENDENTS BOTH.
IT DON'T SEEM RIGHT...
LET'S GET THIS DONE.

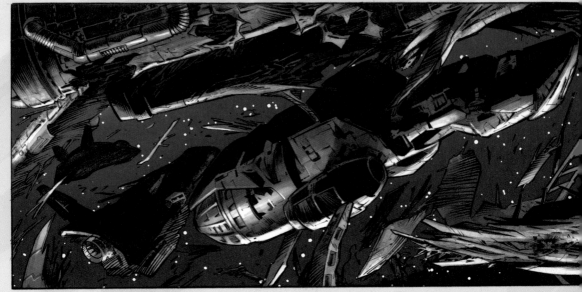

AIRLOCK ESTABLISHED.

PREPARE TO BREACH

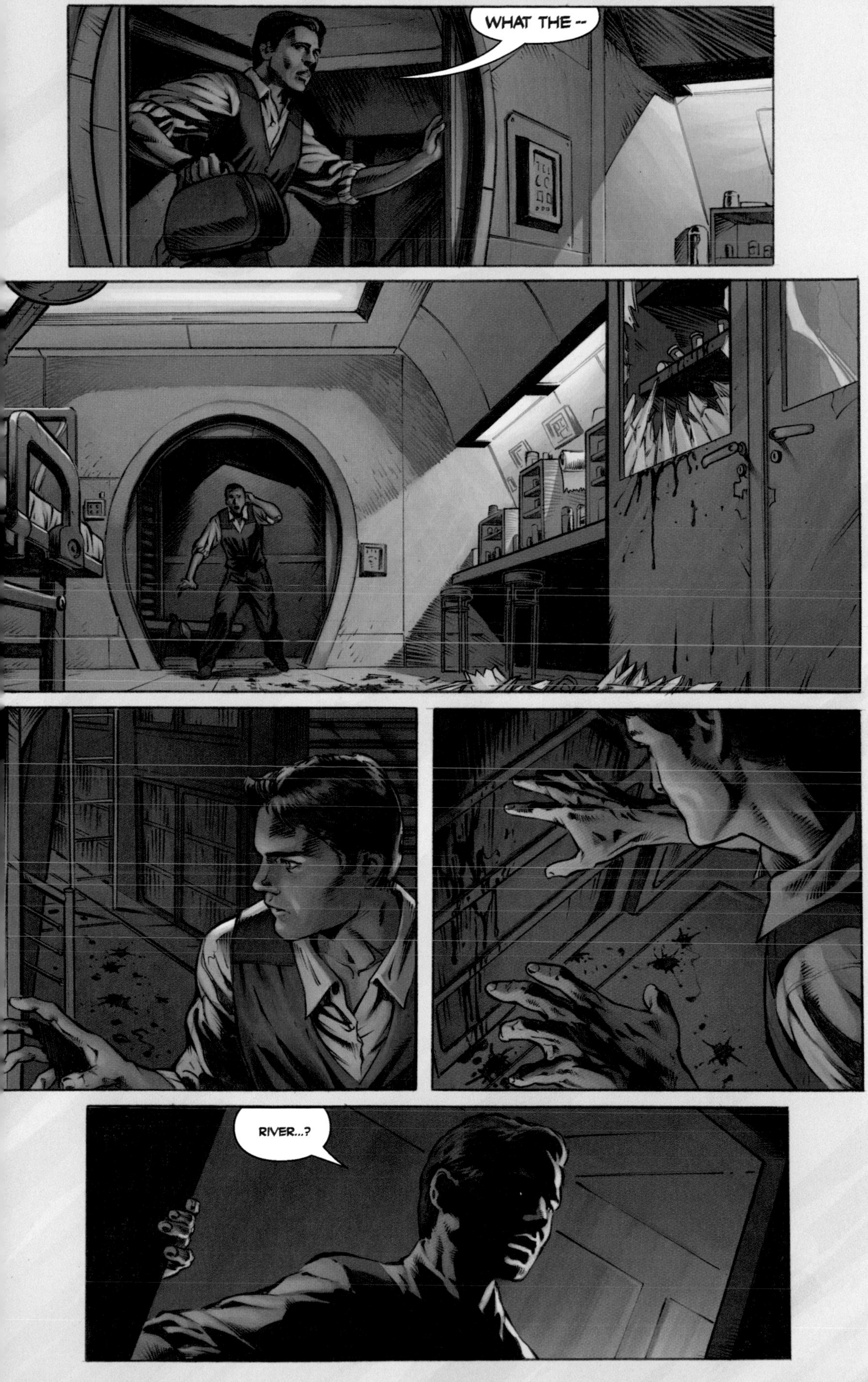
WHAT THE --
RIVER...?

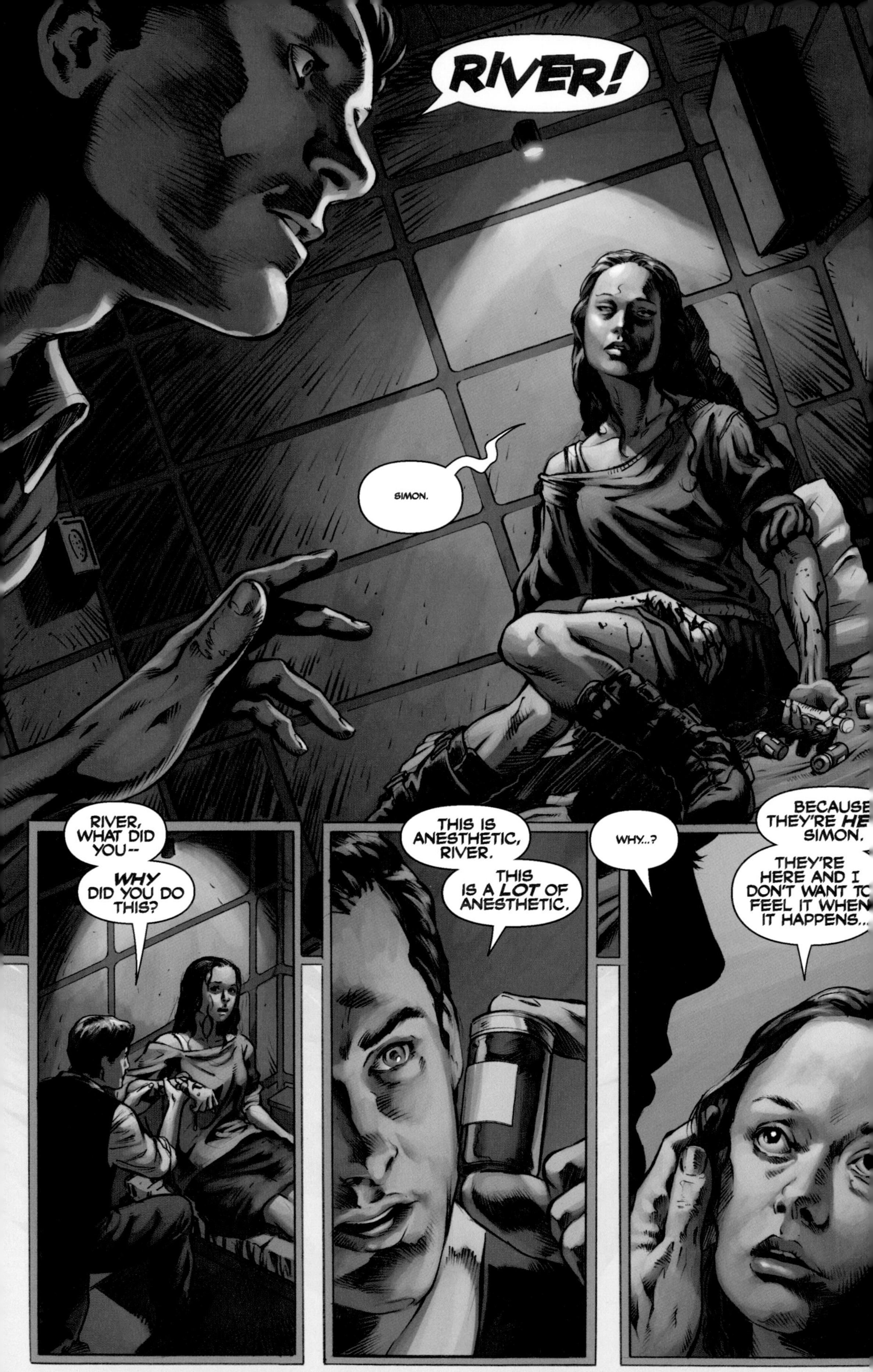
RIVER!
SIMON.
RIVER, WHAT DID YOU--
WHY DID YOU DO THIS?
THIS IS ANESTHETIC, RIVER.
THIS IS A LOT OF ANESTHETIC.
WHY...?
BECAUSE THEY'RE HE SIMON.
THEY'RE HERE AND I DON'T WANT TO FEEL IT WHEN IT HAPPENS...

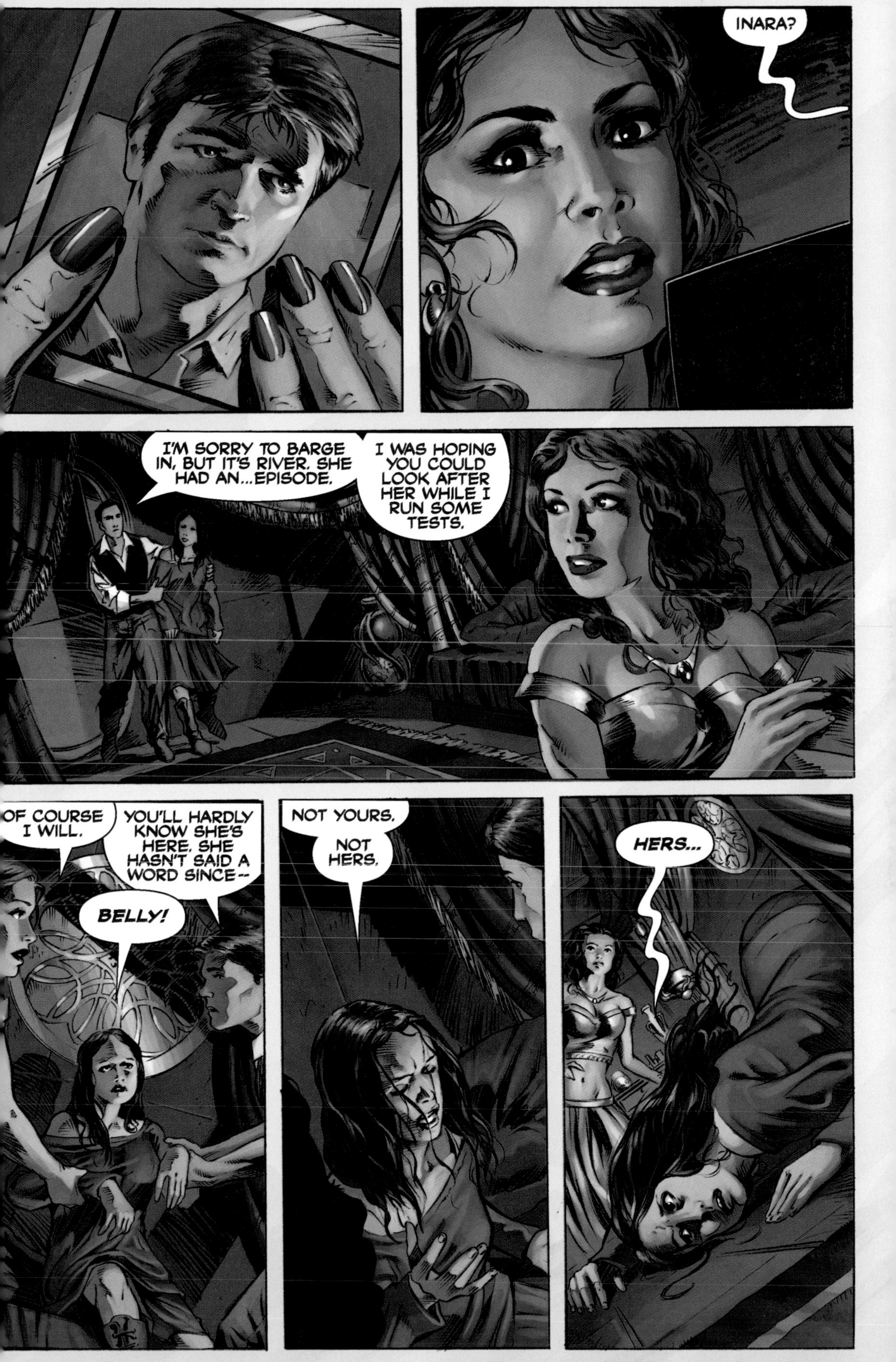
INARA?
I'M SORRY TO BARGE IN, BUT IT'S RIVER. SHE HAD AN...EPISODE.
I WAS HOPING YOU COULD LOOK AFTER HER WHILE I RUN SOME TESTS.
OF COURSE I WILL.
YOU'LL HARDLY KNOW SHE'S HERE. SHE HASN'T SAID A WORD SINCE--
BELLY!
NOT YOURS.
NOT HERS.
HERS...

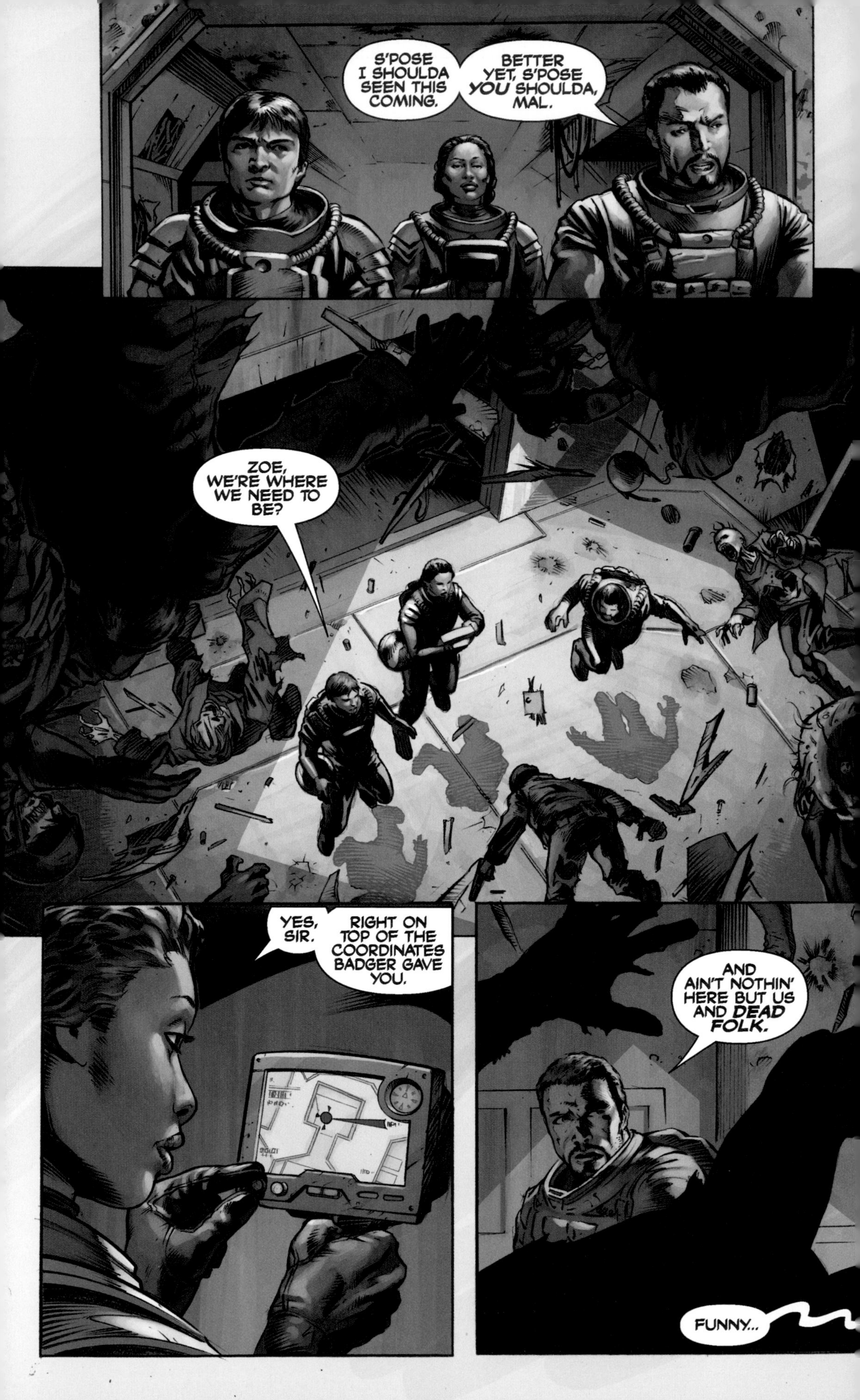
S'POSE I SHOULDA SEEN THIS COMING.
BETTER YET, S'POSE YOU SHOULDA, MAL.
ZOE, WE'RE WHERE WE NEED TO BE?
YES, SIR.
RIGHT ON TOP OF THE COORDINATES BADGER GAVE YOU.
AND AIN'T NOTHIN' HERE BUT US AND DEAD FOLK.
FUNNY...

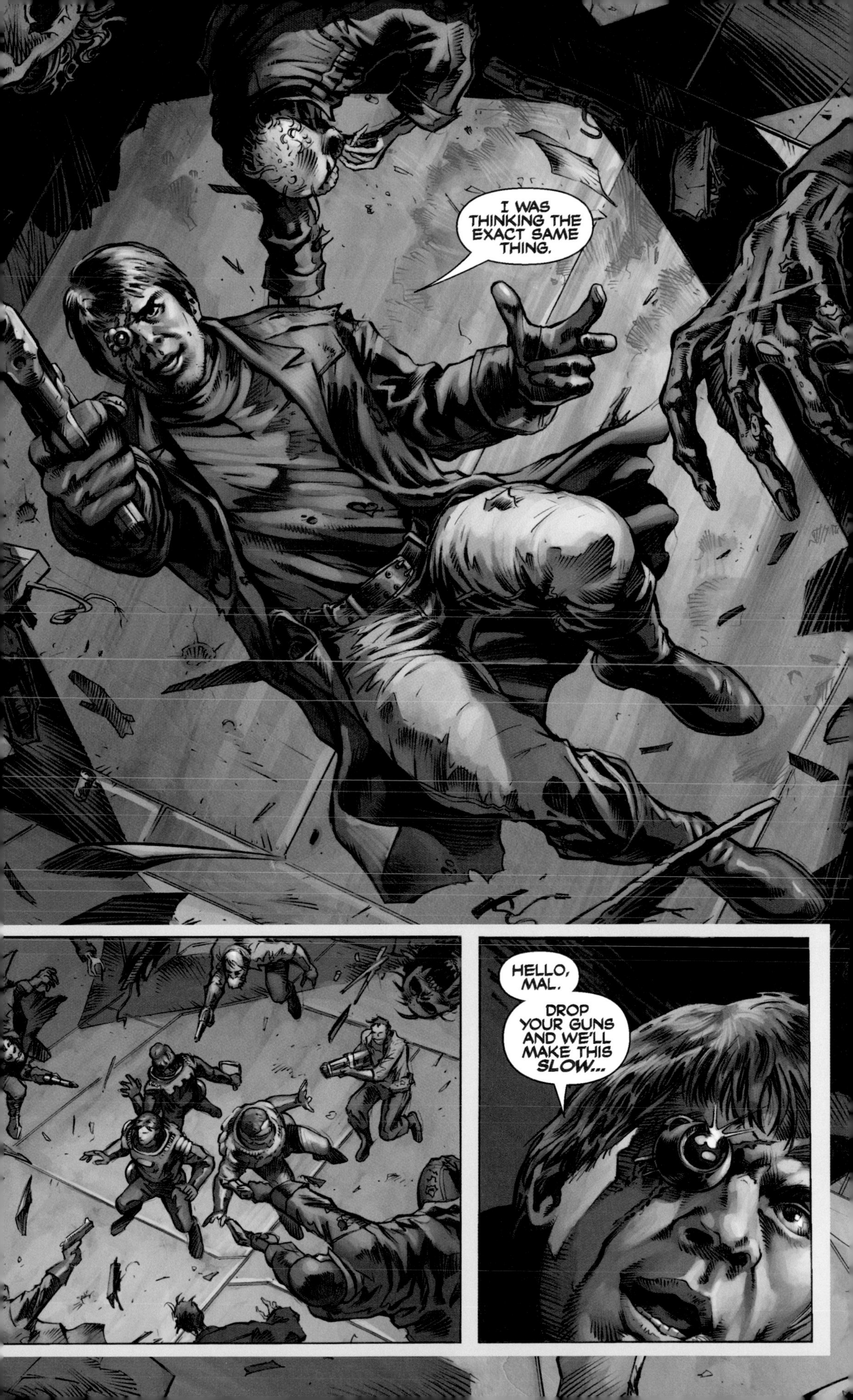
I WAS THINKING THE EXACT SAME THING.
HELLO, MAL.
DROP YOUR GUNS AND WE'LL MAKE THIS *SLOW*...

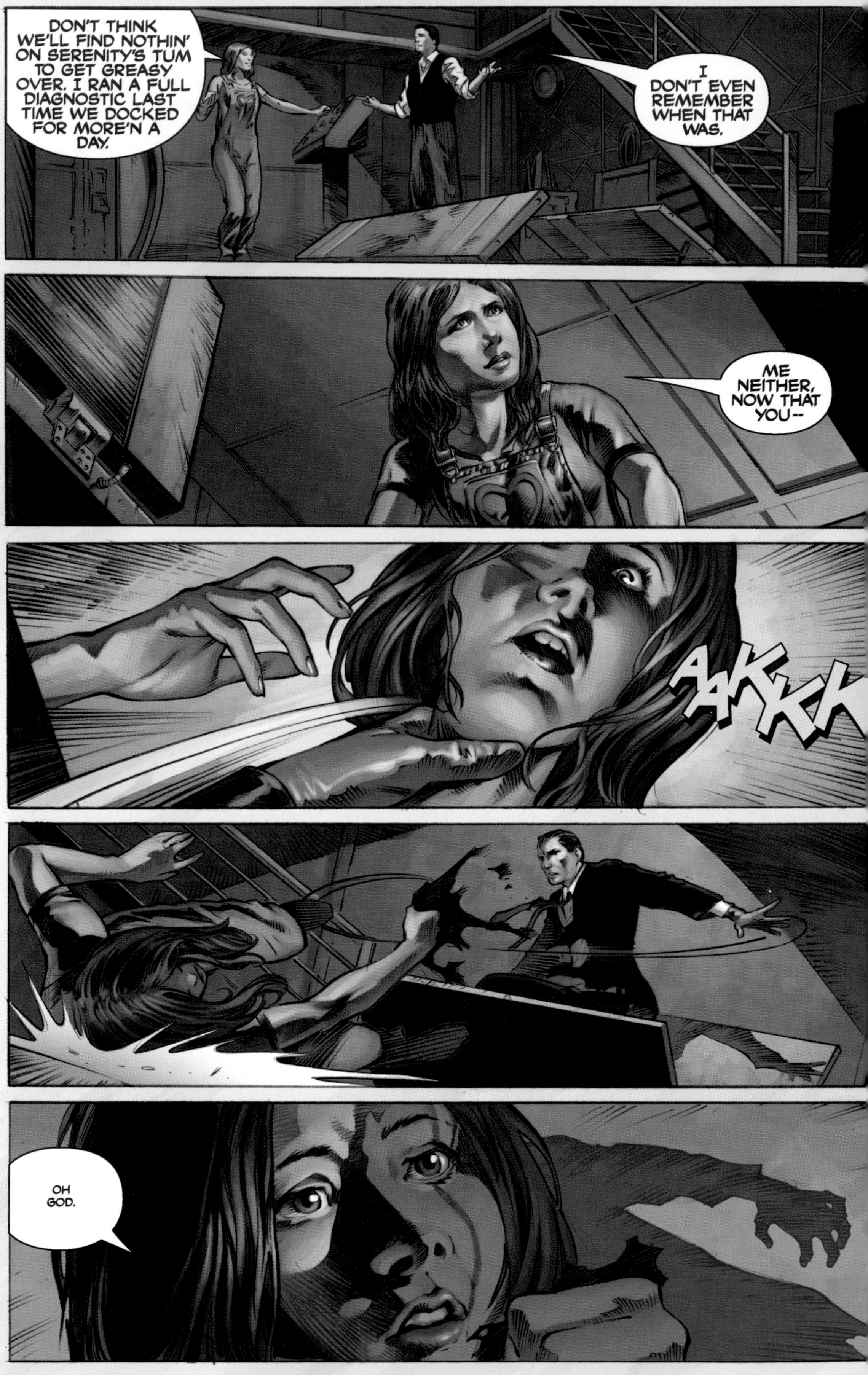
DON'T THINK WE'LL FIND NOTHIN' ON SERENITY'S TUM TO GET GREASY OVER. I RAN A FULL DIAGNOSTIC LAST TIME WE DOCKED FOR MORE'N A DAY.
I DON'T EVEN REMEMBER WHEN THAT WAS.
ME NEITHER, NOW THAT YOU--
AAKKK
OH GOD.

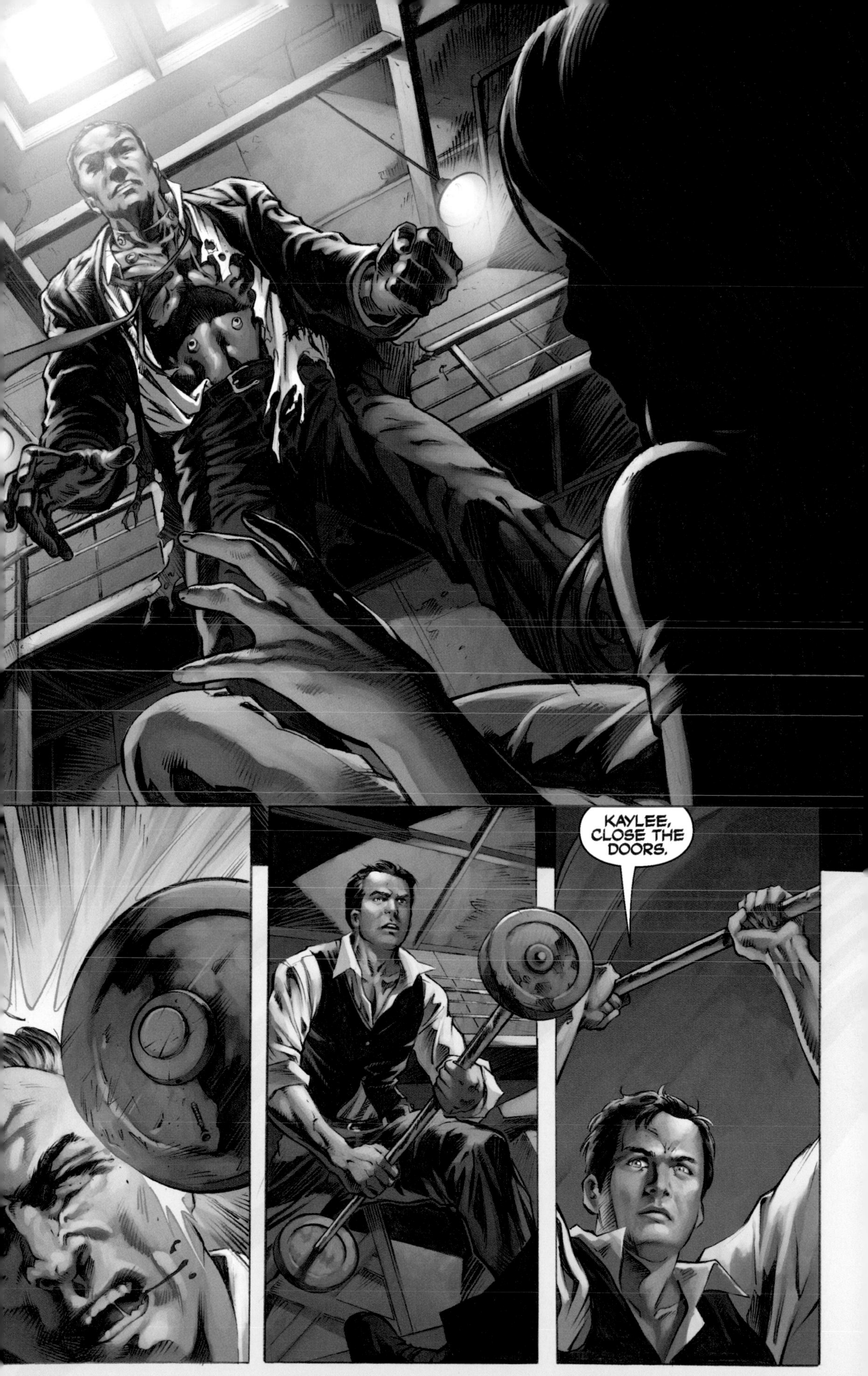
KAYLEE, CLOSE THE DOORS.

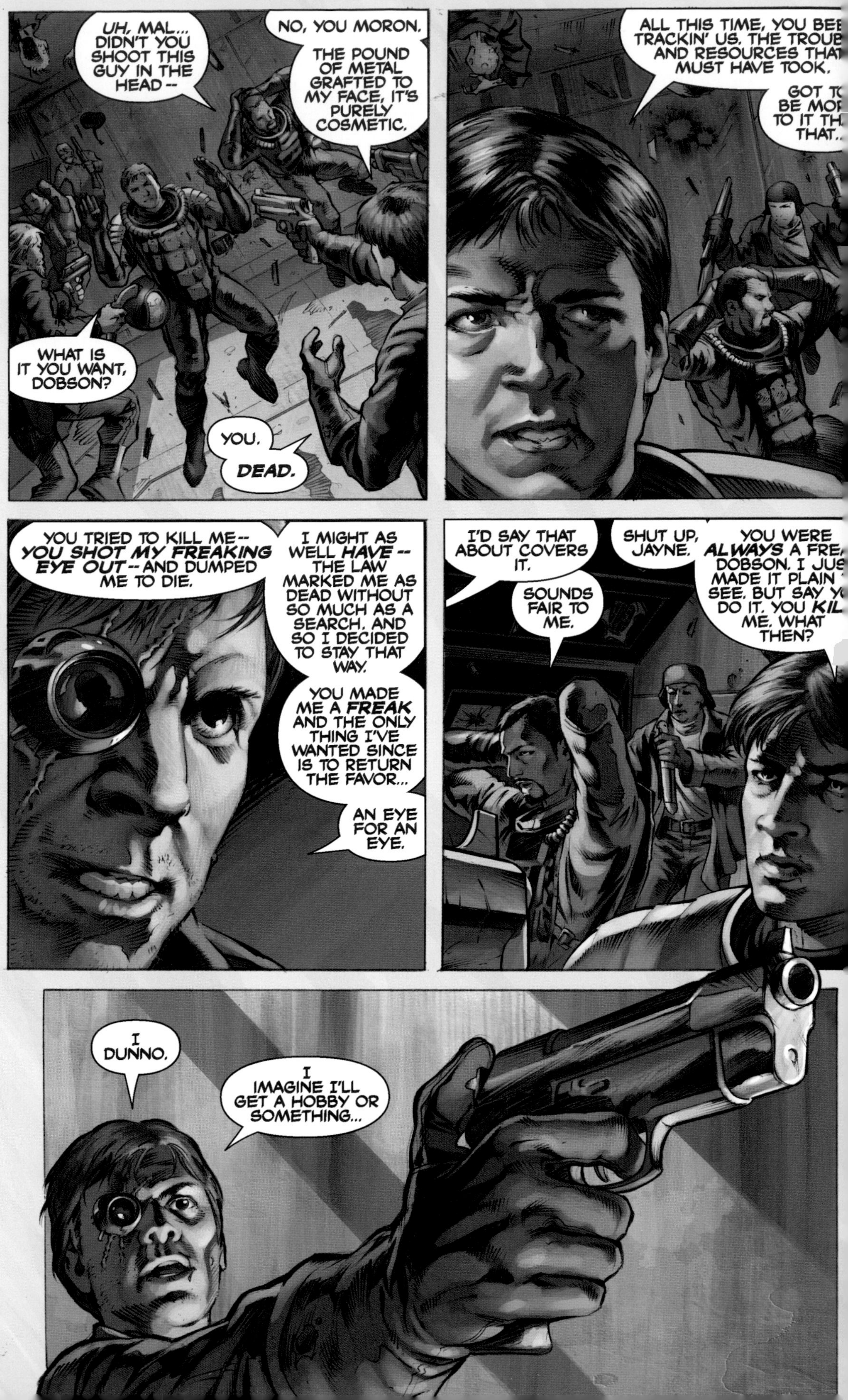
UH, MAL... DIDN'T YOU SHOOT THIS GUY IN THE HEAD --
NO, YOU MORON.
THE POUND OF METAL GRAFTED TO MY FACE, IT'S PURELY COSMETIC.
WHAT IS IT YOU WANT, DOBSON?
YOU.
DEAD.
ALL THIS TIME, YOU BEE TRACKIN' US. THE TROUB AND RESOURCES THA MUST HAVE TOOK.
GOT T BE MO TO IT TH THAT...
YOU TRIED TO KILL ME-- YOU SHOT MY FREAKING EYE OUT -- AND DUMPED ME TO DIE.
I MIGHT AS WELL HAVE -- THE LAW MARKED ME AS DEAD WITHOUT SO MUCH AS A SEARCH. AND SO I DECIDED TO STAY THAT WAY.
YOU MADE ME A FREAK AND THE ONLY THING I'VE WANTED SINCE IS TO RETURN THE FAVOR...
AN EYE FOR AN EYE.
I'D SAY THAT ABOUT COVERS IT.
SOUNDS FAIR TO ME.
SHUT UP, JAYNE.
YOU WERE ALWAYS A FRE DOBSON. I JUS MADE IT PLAIN SEE. BUT SAY Y DO IT. YOU KIL ME. WHAT THEN?
I DUNNO.
I IMAGINE I'LL GET A HOBBY OR SOMETHING...

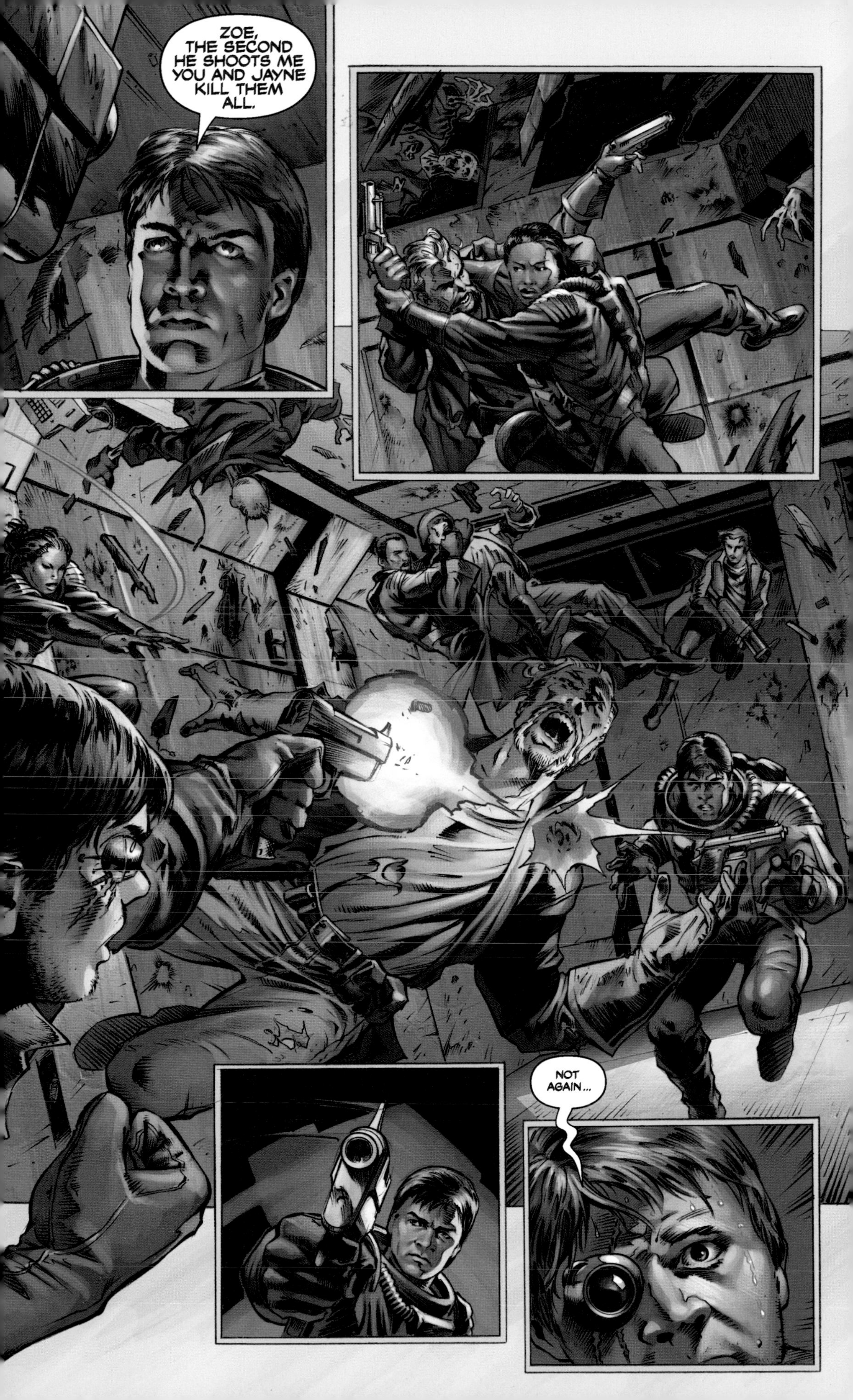
ZOE, THE SECOND HE SHOOTS ME YOU AND JAYNE KILL THEM ALL.
NOT AGAIN...

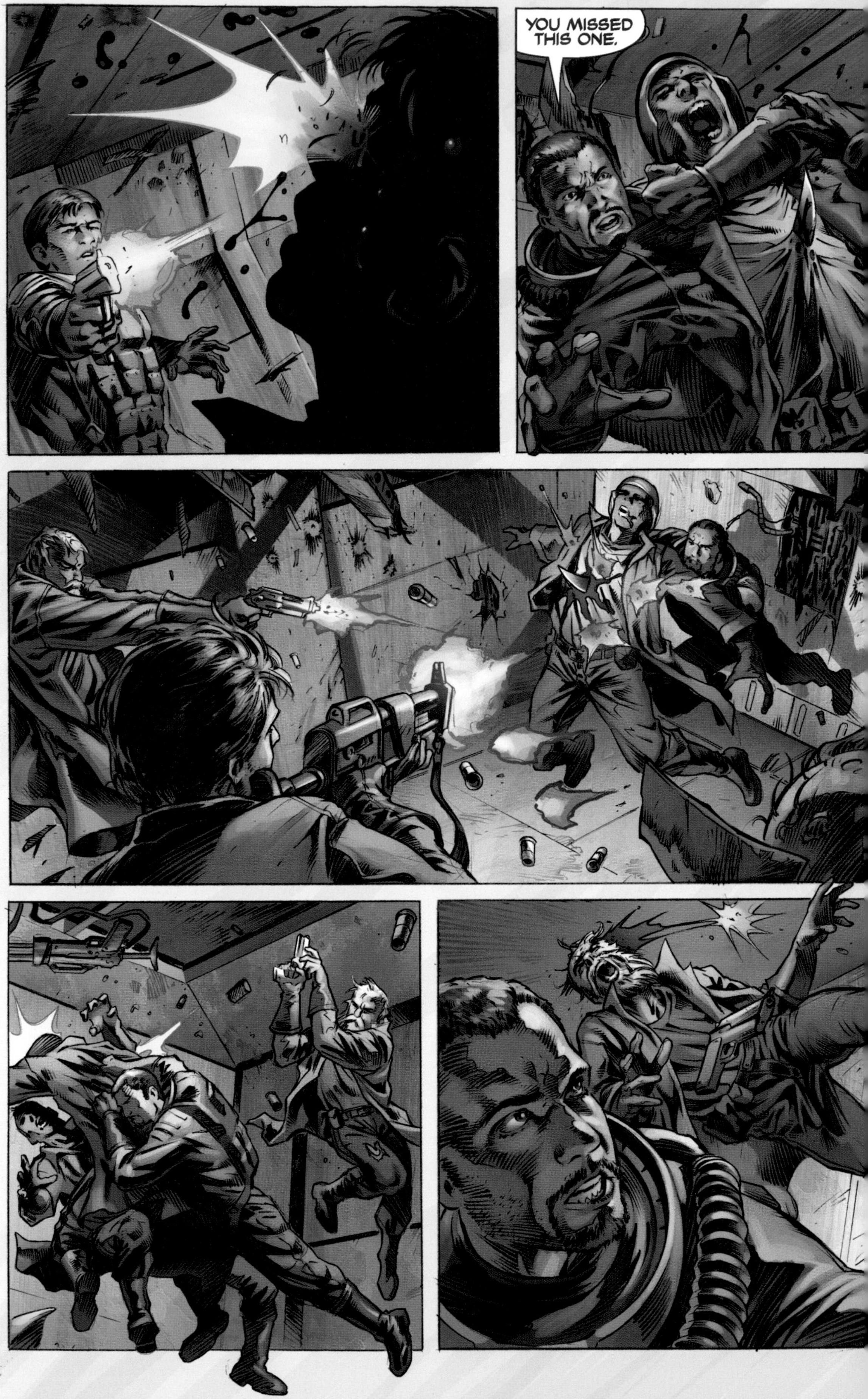
YOU MISSED THIS ONE.

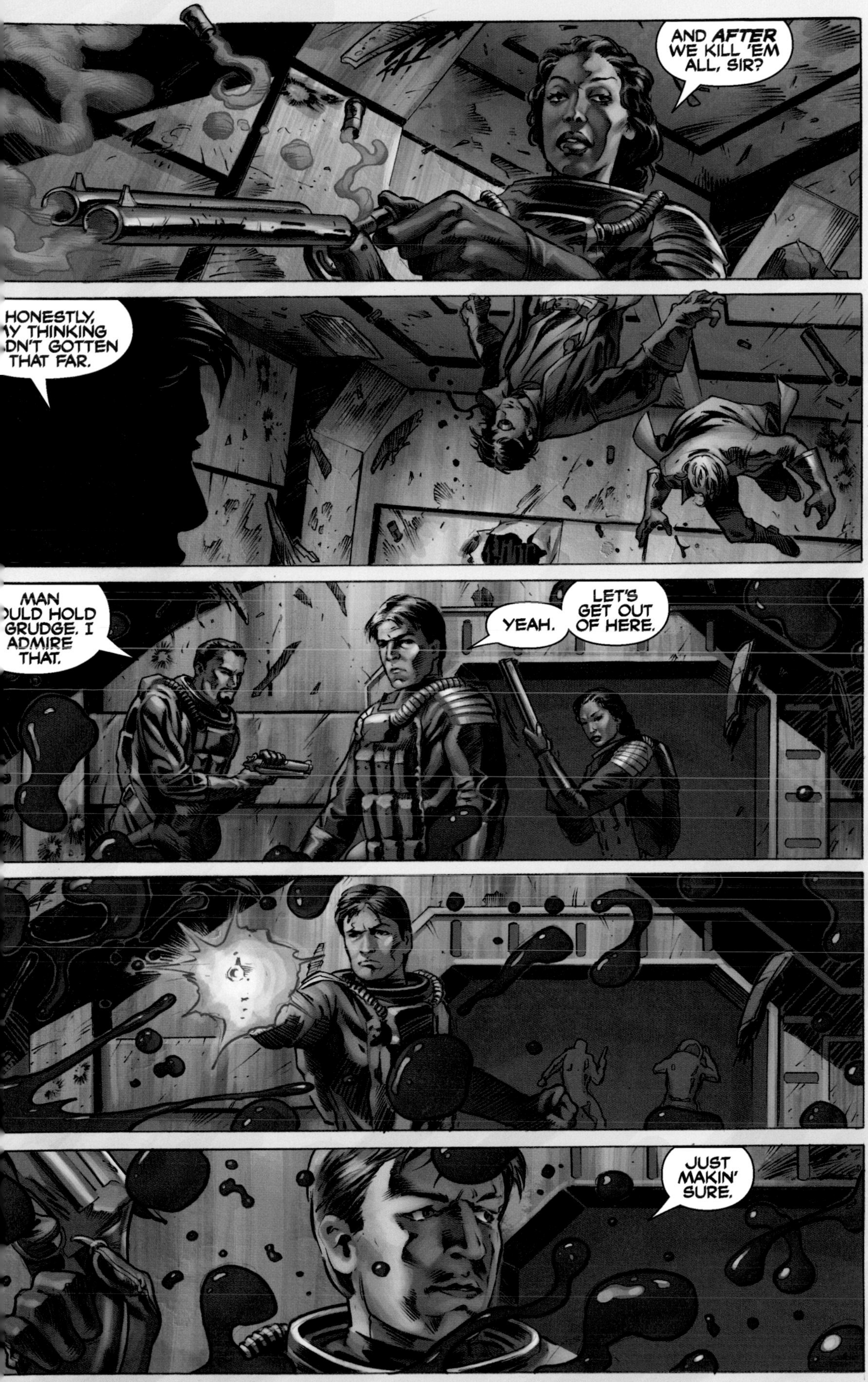
AND AFTER WE KILL 'EM ALL, SIR?
HONESTLY, MY THINKING DN'T GOTTEN THAT FAR.
MAN OULD HOLD GRUDGE. I ADMIRE THAT.
YEAH.
LET'S GET OUT OF HERE.
JUST MAKIN' SURE.

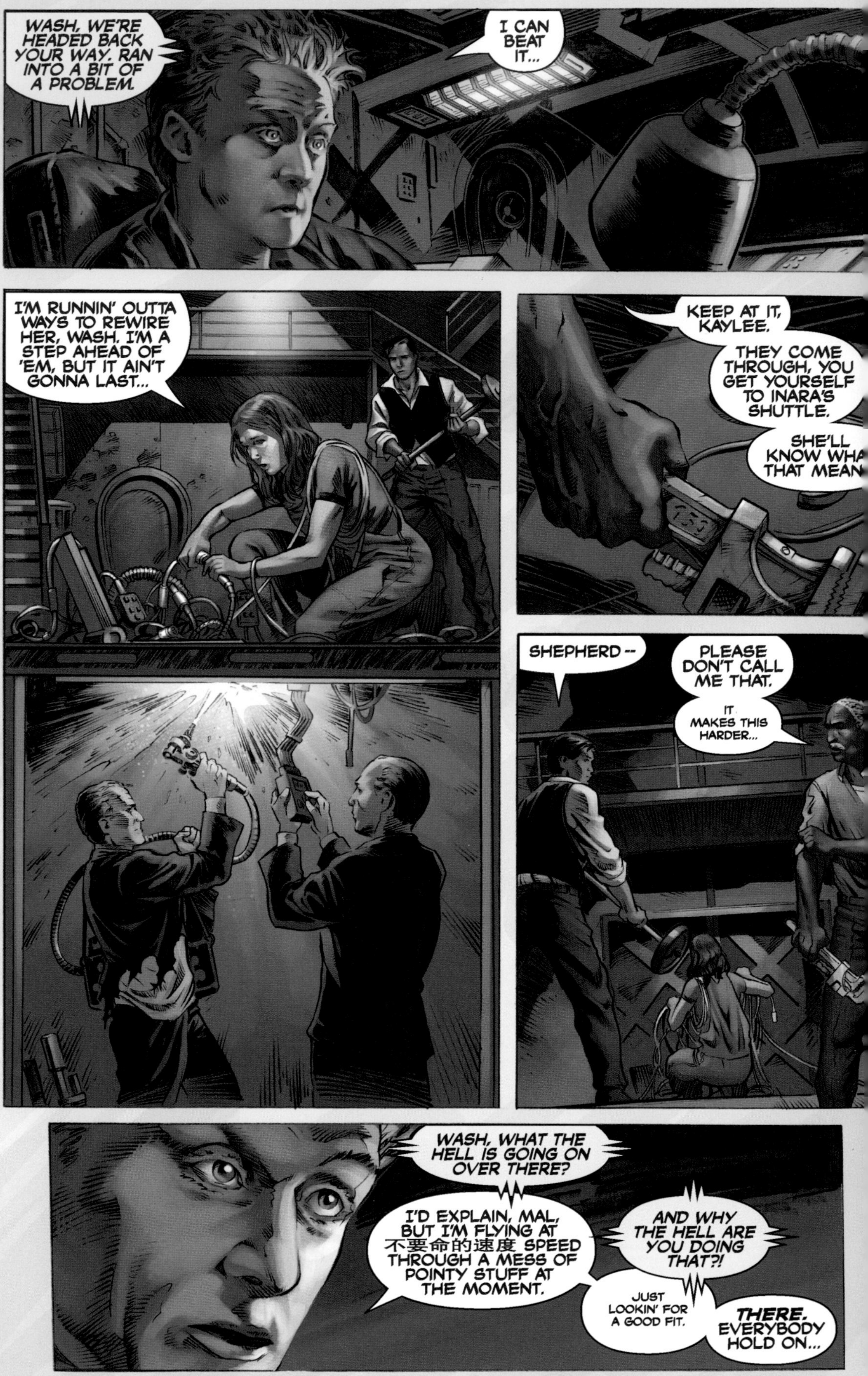
WASH, WE'RE HEADED BACK YOUR WAY. RAN INTO A BIT OF A PROBLEM.
I CAN BEAT IT...
I'M RUNNIN' OUTTA WAYS TO REWIRE HER, WASH. I'M A STEP AHEAD OF 'EM, BUT IT AIN'T GONNA LAST...
KEEP AT IT, KAYLEE.
THEY COME THROUGH, YOU GET YOURSELF TO INARA'S SHUTTLE.
SHE'LL KNOW WHA THAT MEAN
SHEPHERD --
PLEASE DON'T CALL ME THAT.
IT MAKES THIS HARDER...
WASH, WHAT THE HELL IS GOING ON OVER THERE?
I'D EXPLAIN, MAL, BUT I'M FLYING AT 不要命的速度 SPEED THROUGH A MESS OF POINTY STUFF AT THE MOMENT.
AND WHY THE HELL ARE YOU DOING THAT?!
JUST LOOKIN' FOR A GOOD FIT.
THERE. EVERYBODY HOLD ON...

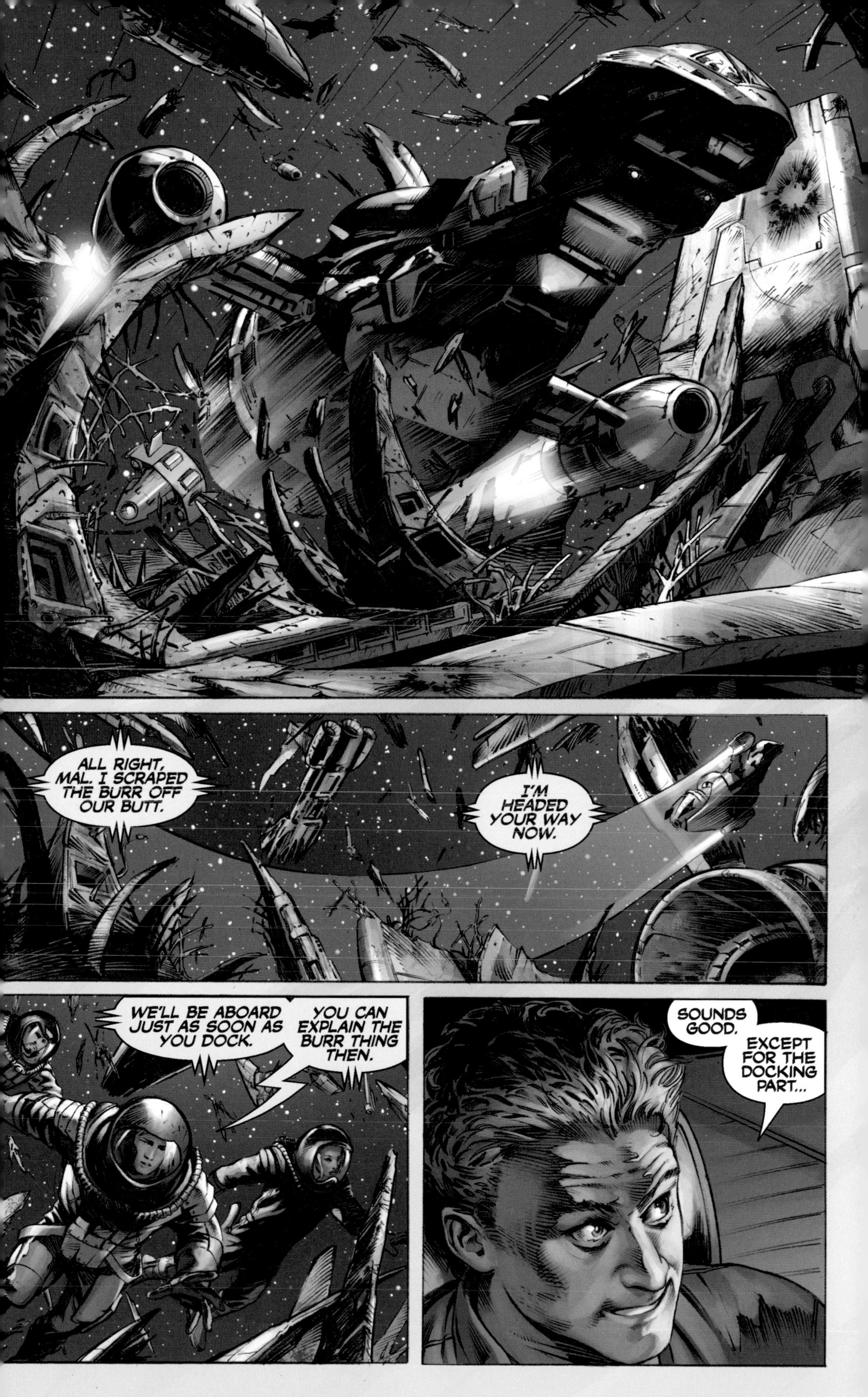
ALL RIGHT, MAL. I SCRAPED THE BURR OFF OUR BUTT.
I'M HEADED YOUR WAY NOW.
WE'LL BE ABOARD JUST AS SOON AS YOU DOCK.
YOU CAN EXPLAIN THE BURR THING THEN.
SOUNDS GOOD,
EXCEPT FOR THE DOCKING PART...

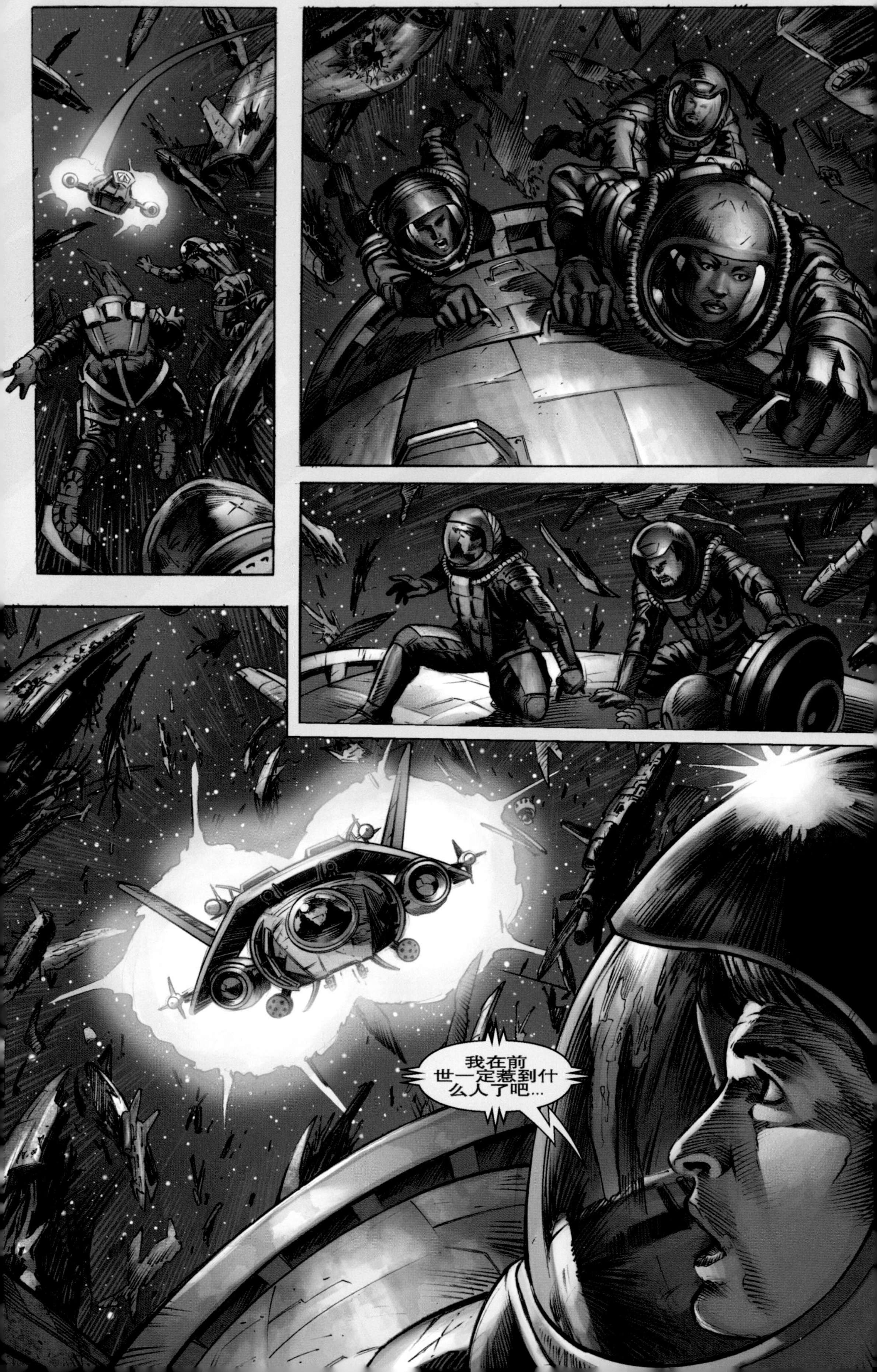
我在前
世一定惹到什
么人了吧...

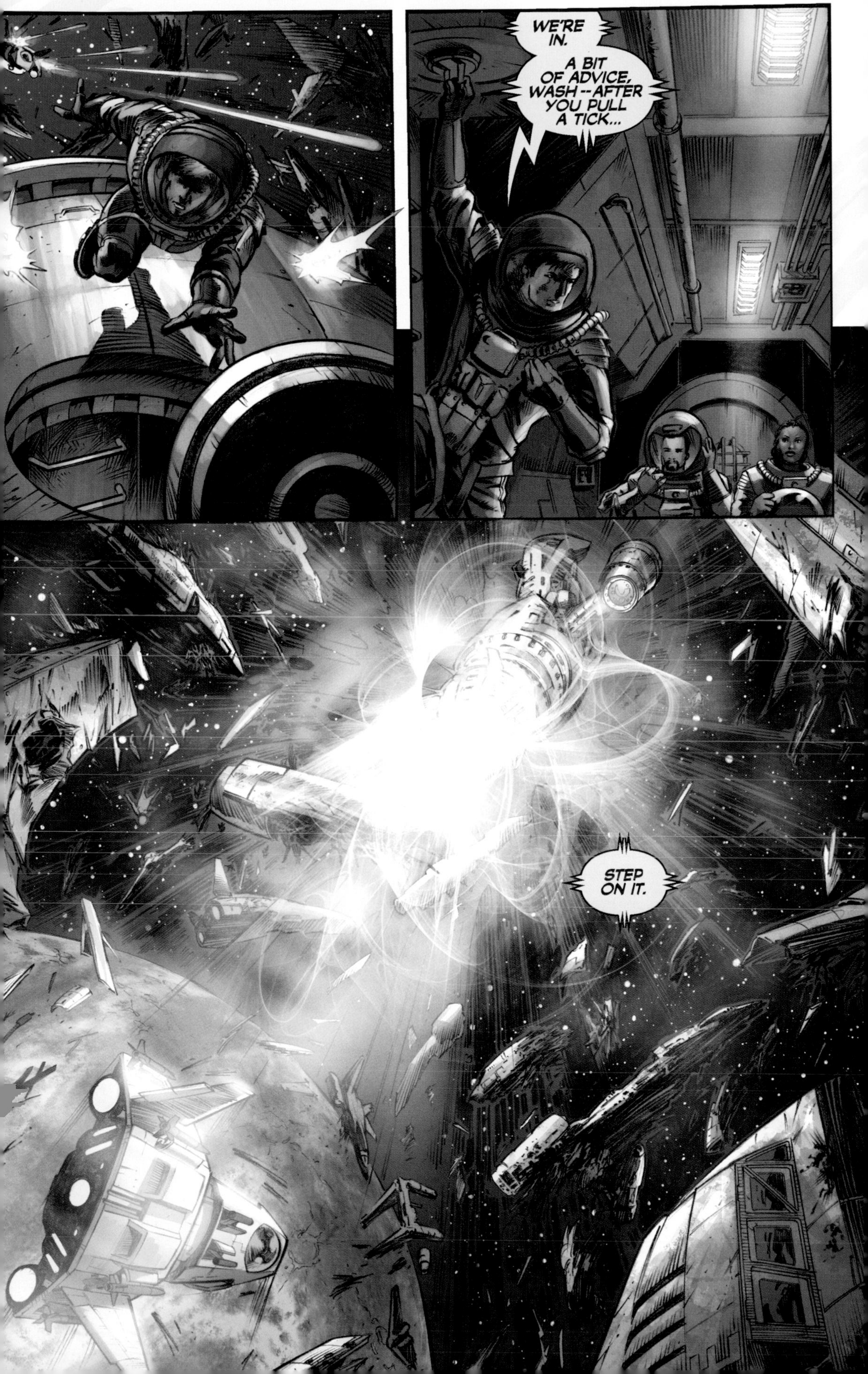
WE'RE IN.
A BIT OF ADVICE, WASH -- AFTER YOU PULL A TICK...
STEP ON IT.

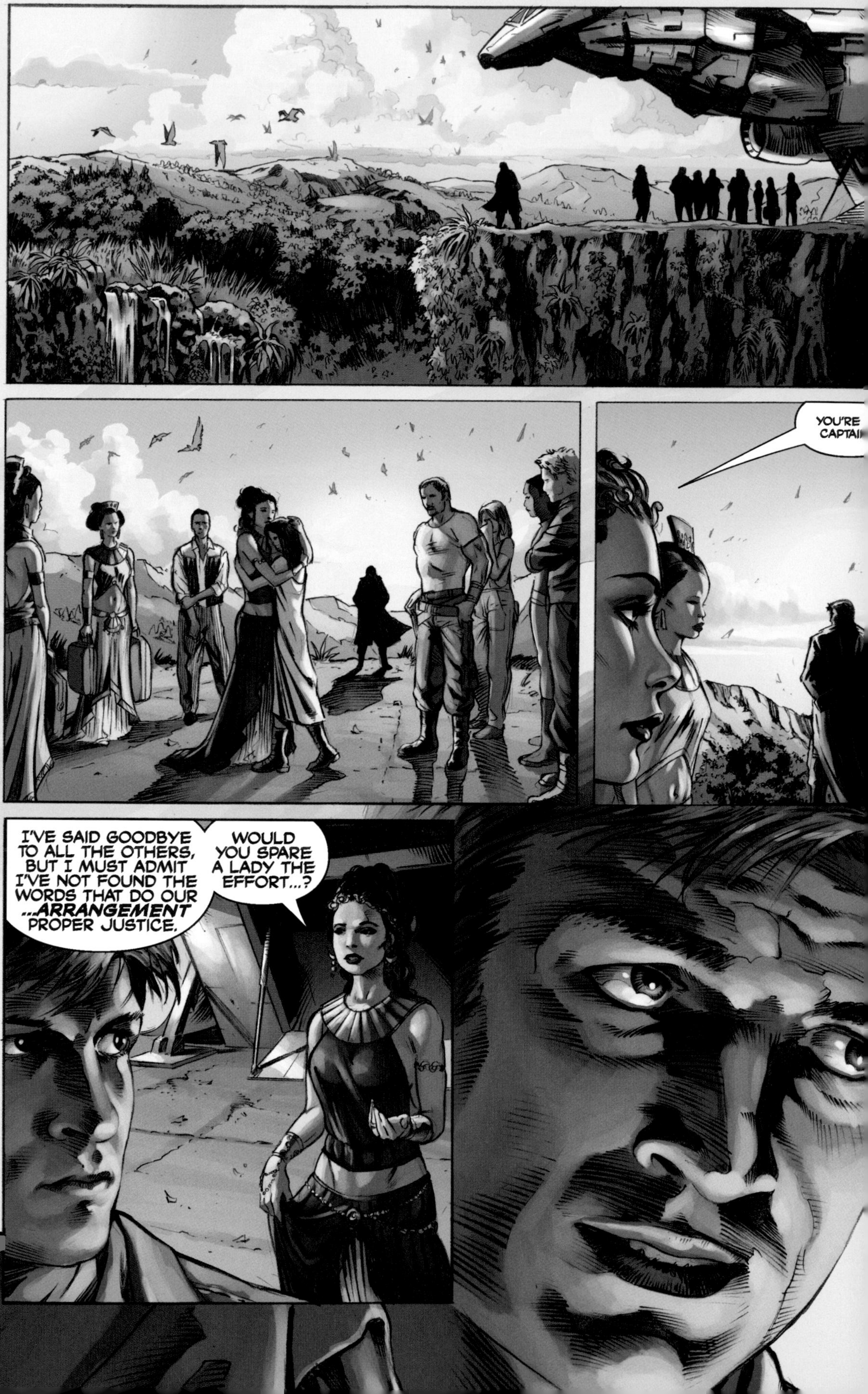
YOU'RE CAPTAI
I'VE SAID GOODBYE TO ALL THE OTHERS, BUT I MUST ADMIT I'VE NOT FOUND THE WORDS THAT DO OUR ...ARRANGEMENT PROPER JUSTICE.
WOULD YOU SPARE A LADY THE EFFORT...?

I'LL MISS YOU, INARA.

I KEEP COMING UP WITH ALL MANNER OF THINGS TO SAY BUT THAT'S WHAT THEY ALL MEAN, IT COMES RIGHT DOWN TO IT.

I DON'T WANT YOU TO --

AM I INTERRUPTING SOMETHING, CAPTAIN?

NOT THAT I KNOW WHAT THAT WOULD BE, YOU STANDING HERE ALONE IN THE MIDDLE OF THE NIGHT.

WE'RE IN SPACE, SHEPHERD. IT'S ALWAYS THE MIDDLE OF THE NIGHT.

WHAT'S ON YOUR MIND?

I'M LEAVING THE SHIP.

DON'T KNOW WHERE FOR JUST YET, BUT IT'S TIME FOR ME TO MOVE ON. I THOUGHT YOU SHOULD BE THE FIRST TO KNOW.

LOOK, SHEPHERD, ... I'LL MAKE THIS PLAIN...

IT DON'T MATTER TO ME THAT YOU HIT ME.

WHICH IS EXACTLY WHY I NEED TO BE AWAY FROM YOU.

BECAUSE SOONER OR LATER, IT WON'T MATTER TO ME, EITHER.

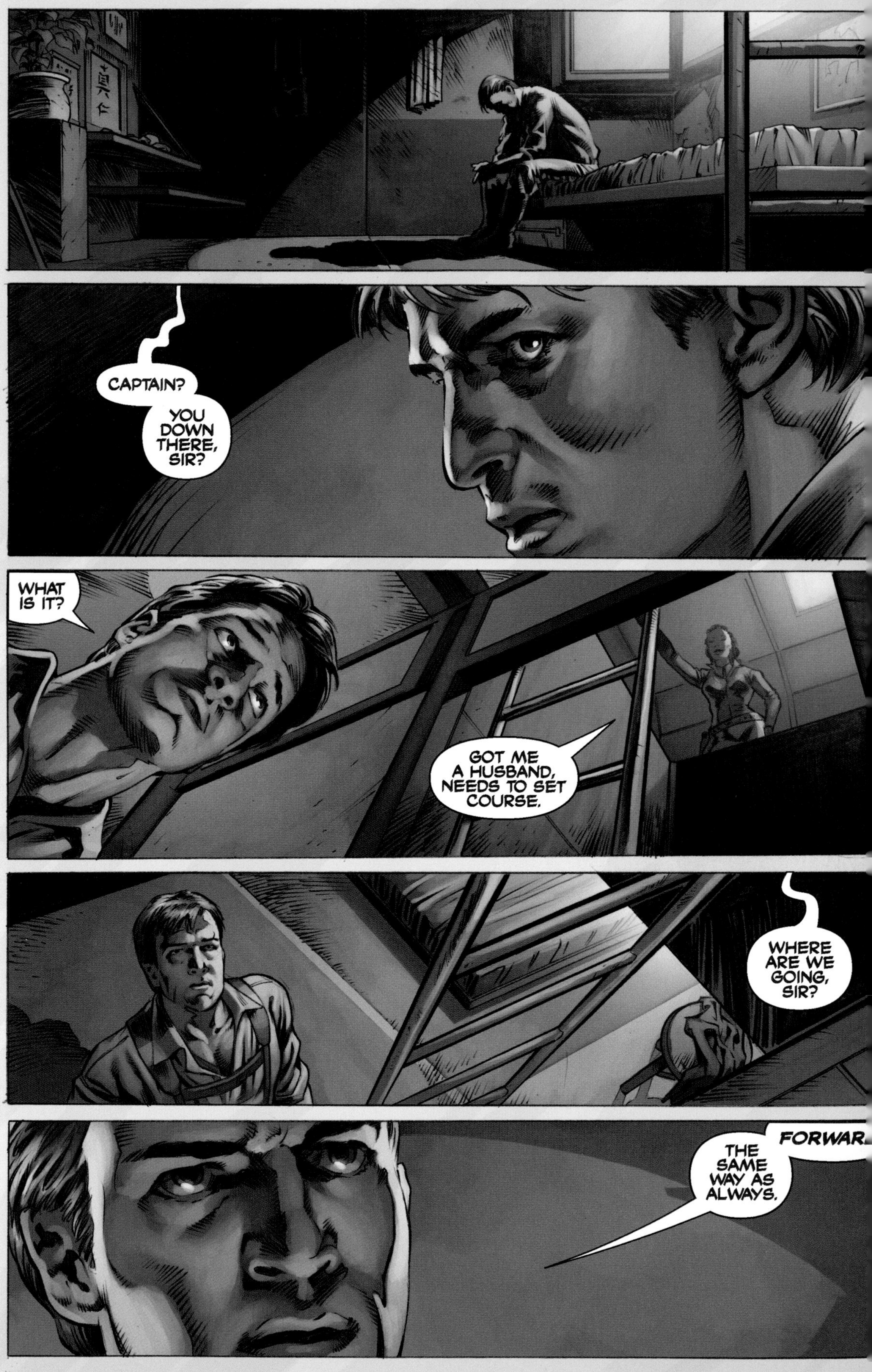
CAPTAIN?
YOU DOWN THERE, SIR?
WHAT IS IT?
GOT ME A HUSBAND, NEEDS TO SET COURSE.
WHERE ARE WE GOING, SIR?
THE SAME WAY AS ALWAYS.
FORWAR

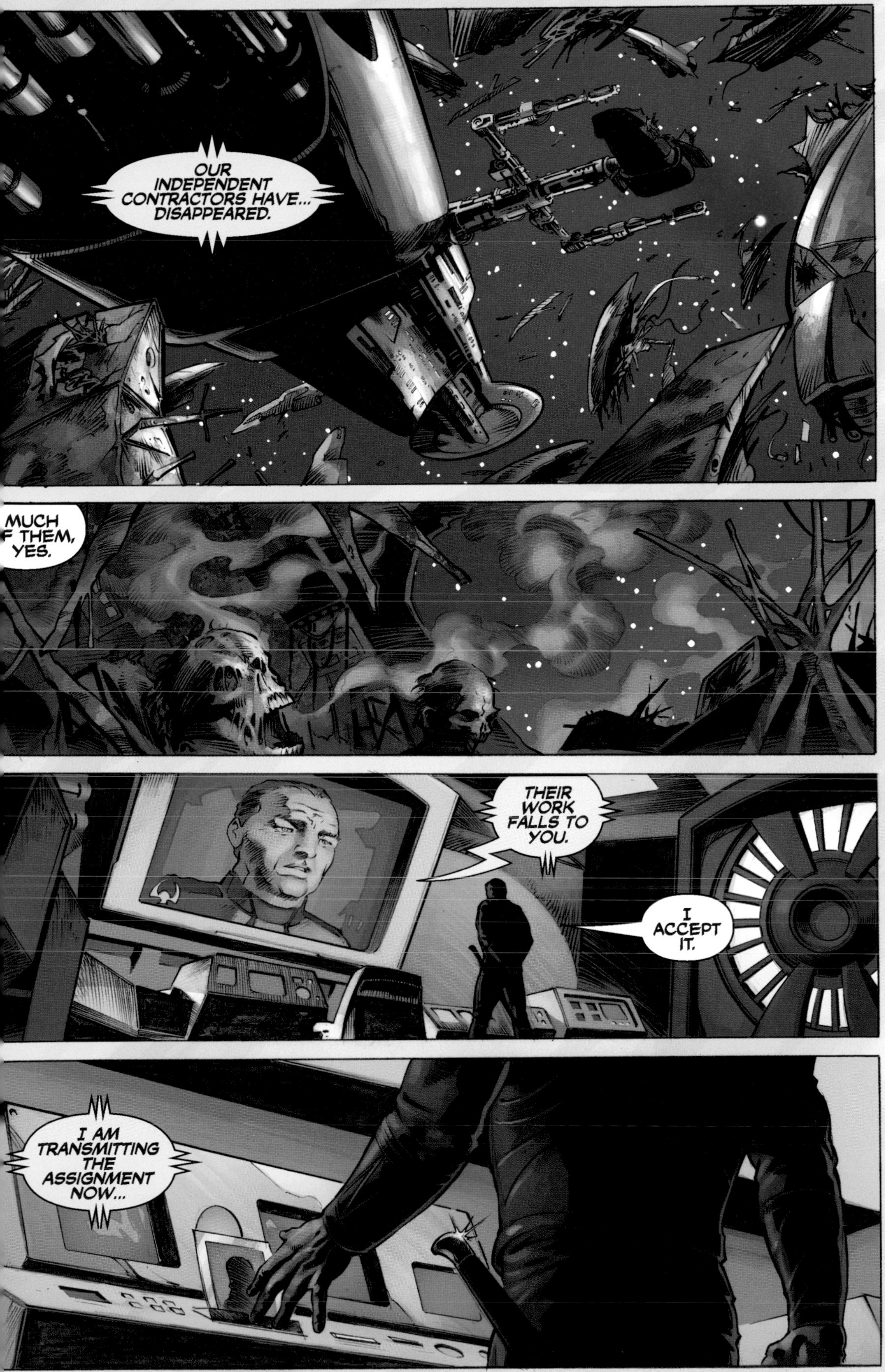
OUR INDEPENDENT CONTRACTORS HAVE... DISAPPEARED.
MUCH F THEM, YES.
THEIR WORK FALLS TO YOU.
I ACCEPT IT.
I AM TRANSMITTING THE ASSIGNMENT NOW...

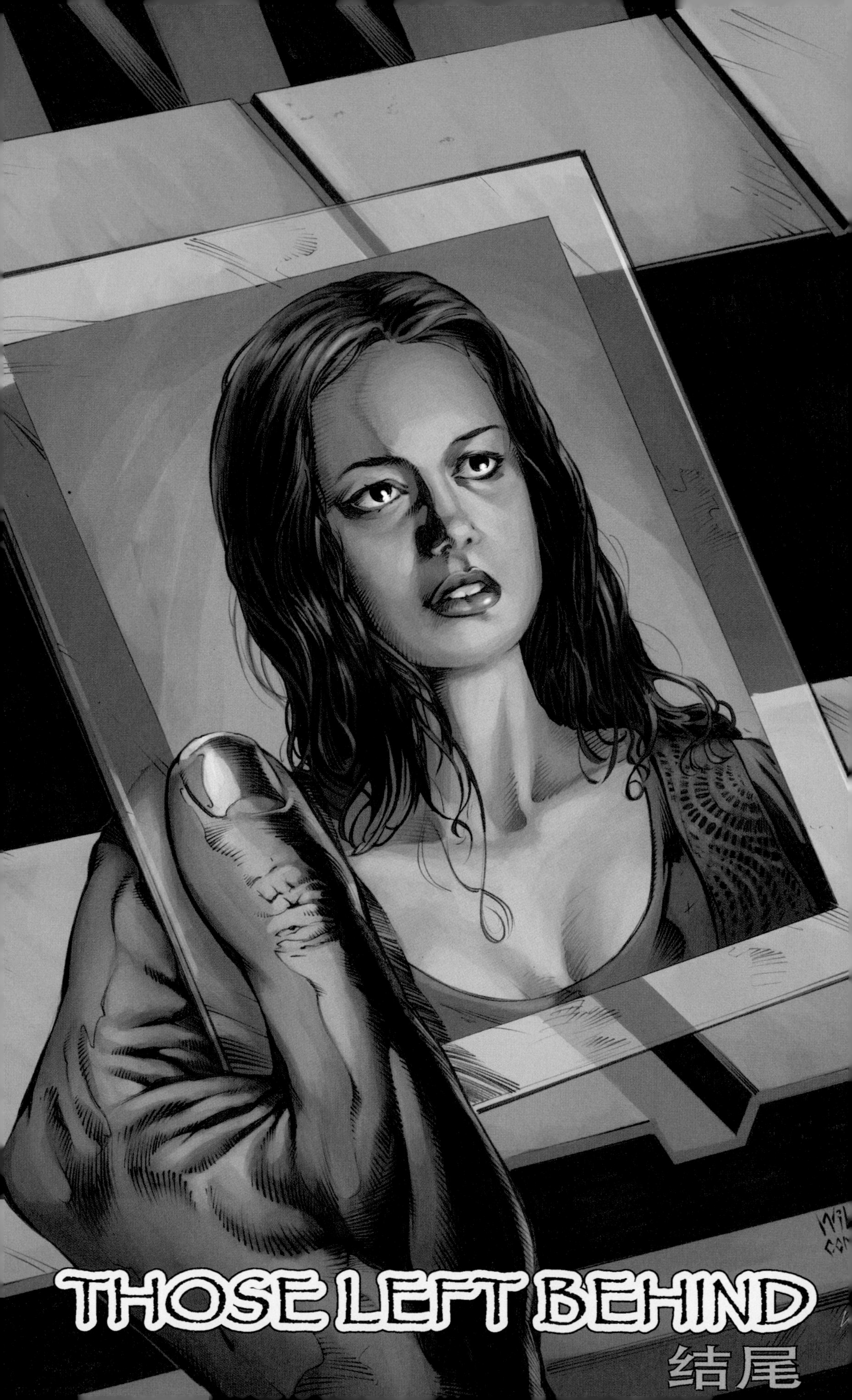
THOSE LEFT BEHIND
结尾

Serenity

宁静 FIREFLY CLASS 03-K64™

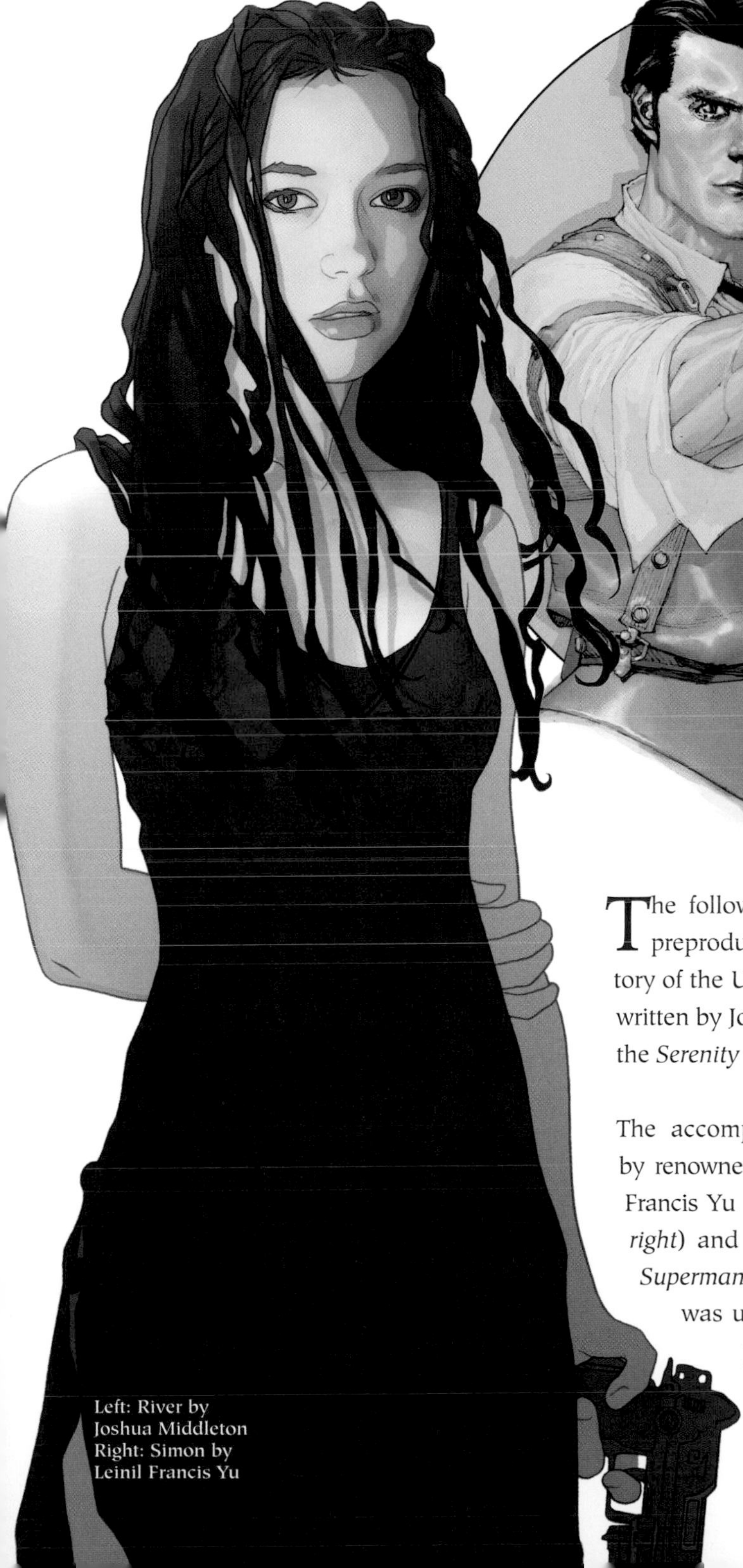

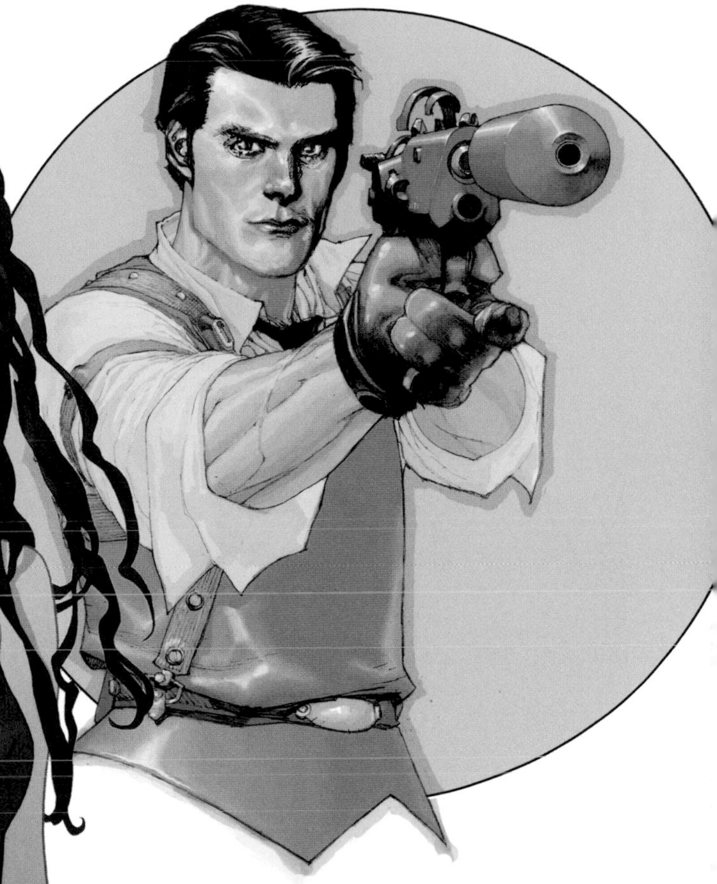

The following section contains the preproduction memo "A Brief History of the Universe, Circa 2516 A.D." written by Joss Whedon for use during the *Serenity* motion picture.

The accompanying artwork, created by renowned comic-book artists Leinil Francis Yu (*X-Men*; *Superman: Birthright*) and Joshua Middleton (*NYX*; *Superman/Shazam: First Thunder*), was used as concept art during preproduction of the film *Serenity*. They also contributed variant covers to the comic-book series.

Left: River by Joshua Middleton
Right: Simon by Leinil Francis Yu

A BRIEF HISTORY OF THE UNIVERSE, Circa 2516 A.D.

By Joss Whedon

Earth-That-Was couldn't handle the growing population and resource needs of humankind. Amazingly enough, instead of wiping itself out, the human race rose to the challenge of finding a new home for the species. A nearby star was located, home to dozens of planets and hundreds of moons, almost all of which had enough mass and solidity to be templates for new Earths. Through giant atmosphere processing plants, terraforming technologies, gravity regulation, and the introduction of every known form of Earthlife, each planet became its own little (or in some cases, huge) Earth. Every person willing and able to leave the Earth migrated to the new system. An entire generation never even saw the outside of a spaceship; the journey took so long. But the planets were ready for habitation (despite the odd quirk of nature or miscalculation on a few) and civilization as we knew it began to rebuild. The work started on the two largest, most central planets, SIHNON and LONDINIUM.

On Earth-That-Was, the two ruling powers were once known as America and China. Though their empires remained separate, the two powers worked together throughout the colonization process, their cultures—as so many had—melding at many levels. Londinium, called so after the Roman name for England's capital (a country long before annexed by America in a somewhat ironic reversal), represented what was once the

Concept art for the
interior of the Companion
Training House by Joshua Middleton

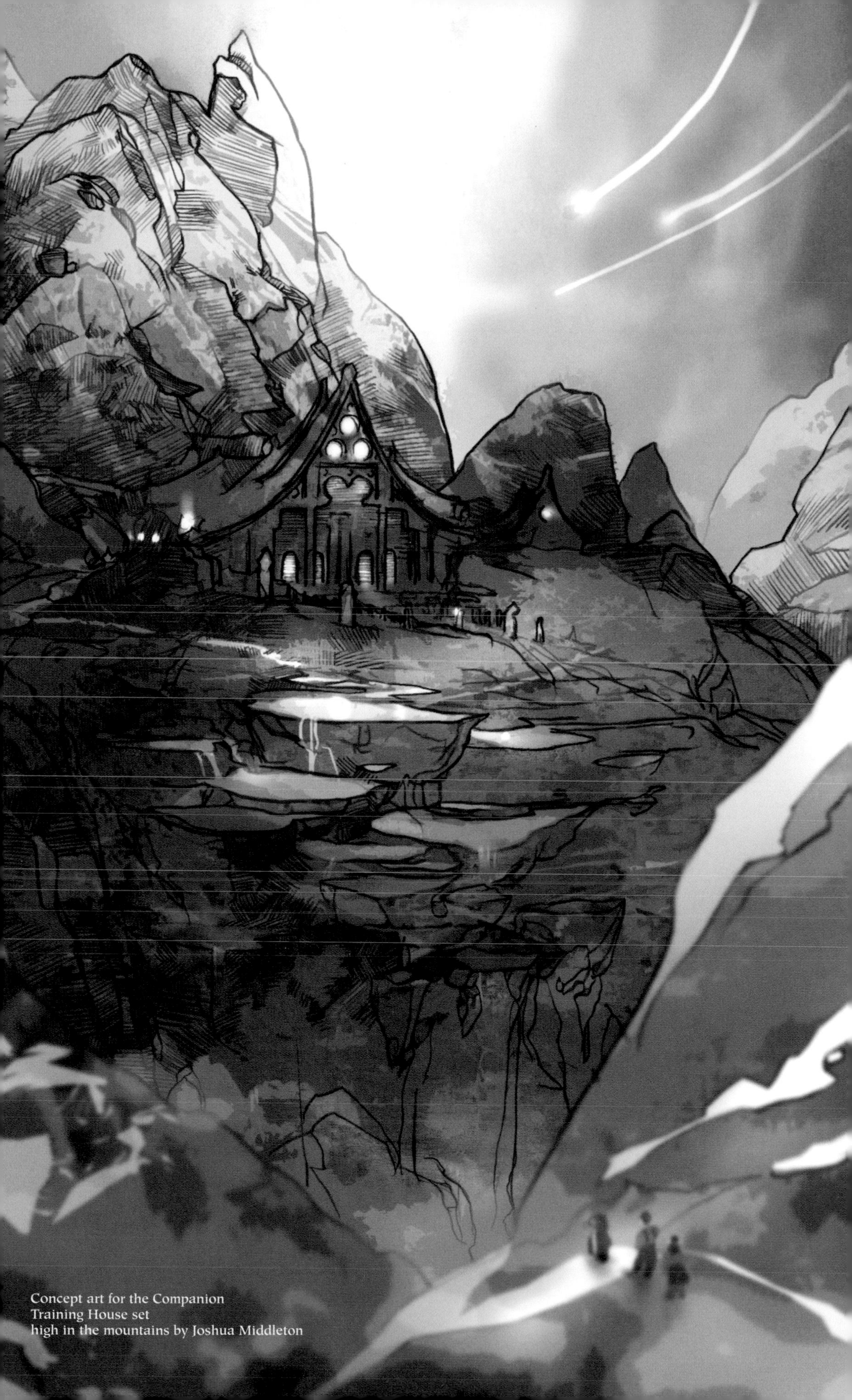

Concept art for the Companion
Training House set
high in the mountains by Joshua Middleton

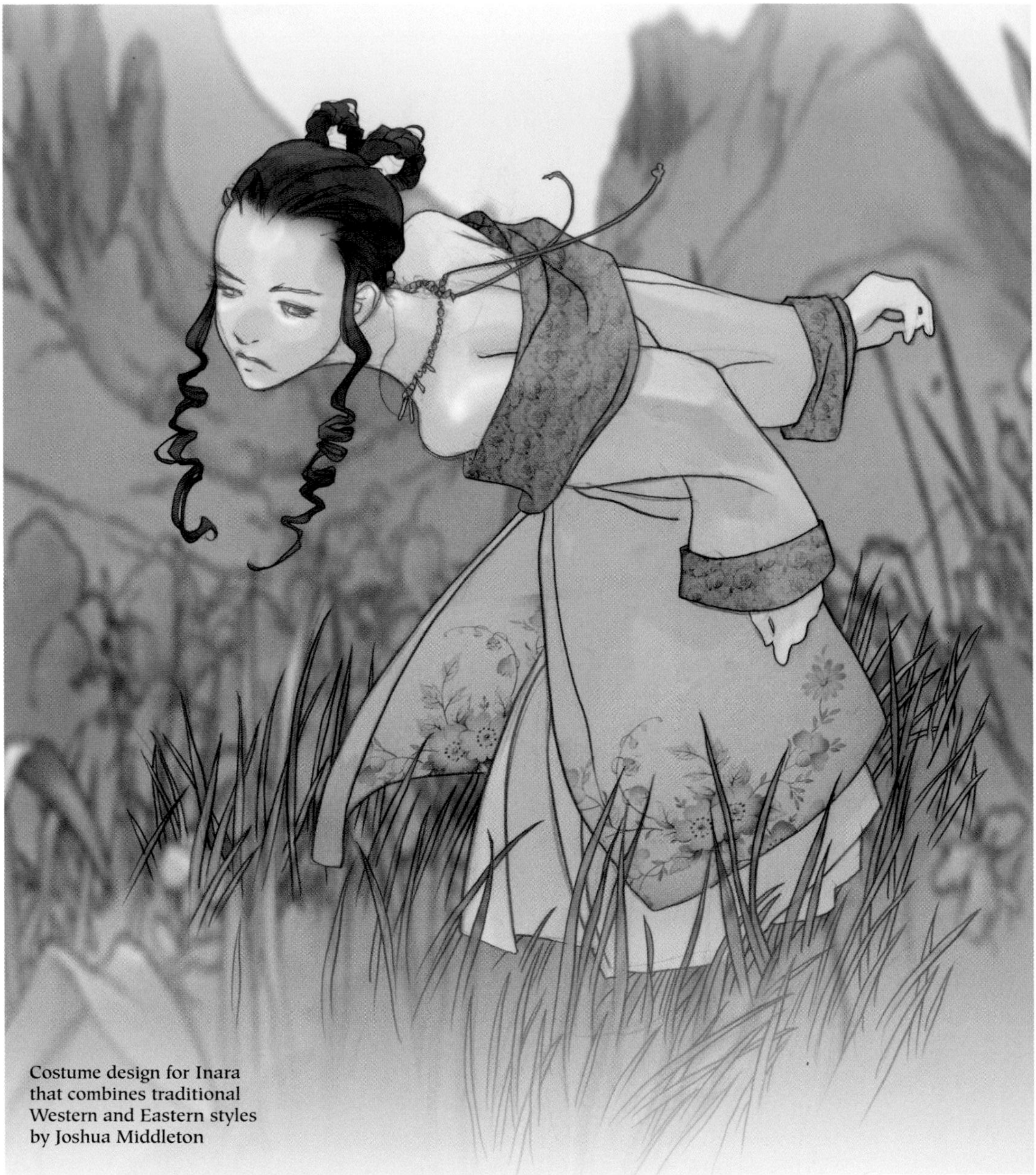

Costume design for Inara that combines traditional Western and Eastern styles by Joshua Middleton

American Empire. Sihnon ("SEE-non," a bastardization of Sino, our word for "Chinese") was the new China, basically. These two powers, still working in harmony, grew at once into the most populous and advanced civilizations in the new galaxy.

"Advanced" meant just that: these were enlightened cultures, with respect for all non-aggressive religious beliefs (though the main religion on both planets was Buddhism). Literacy levels were at 94 percent. Average lifespan was 120. Public service was not law—it was simply an ingrained part of the people's ethos. And pot was totally legal (though I probably won't stress that. In fact, forget I said it). The point is, certain social mores had evolved (whether forward or backward is a matter of opinion) beyond our modern conceptions. As, for example, sex. Prostitution as we understand it had long since been abolished by the legalization and strict federal regulation of the sex trade. "Companion" houses were set up throughout the central planets. No house could ever be run by a man. No Companion could ever be coerced into accepting a client. Companions trained in all the arts; they were extremely well schooled. They lived not

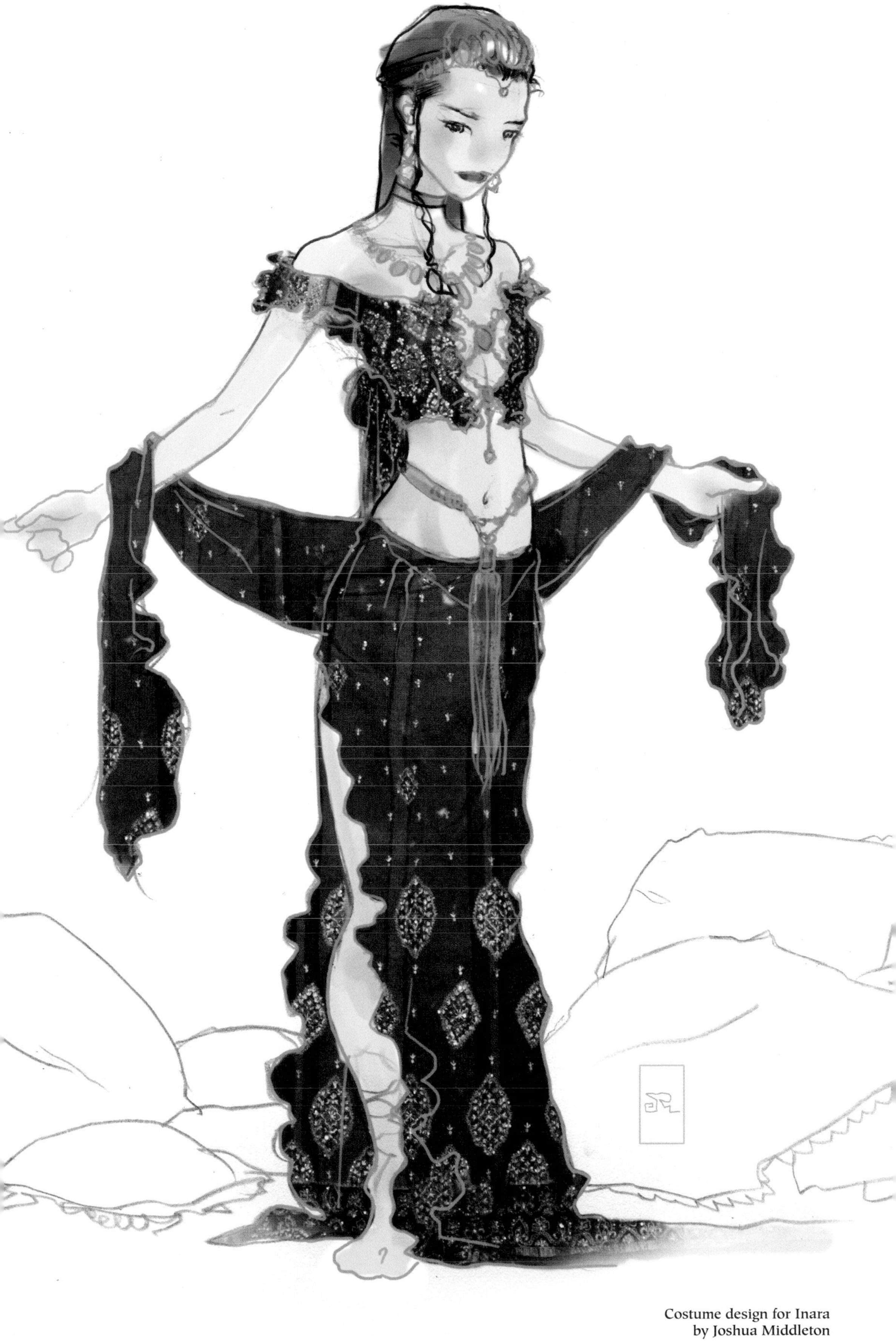

Costume design for Inara
by Joshua Middleton

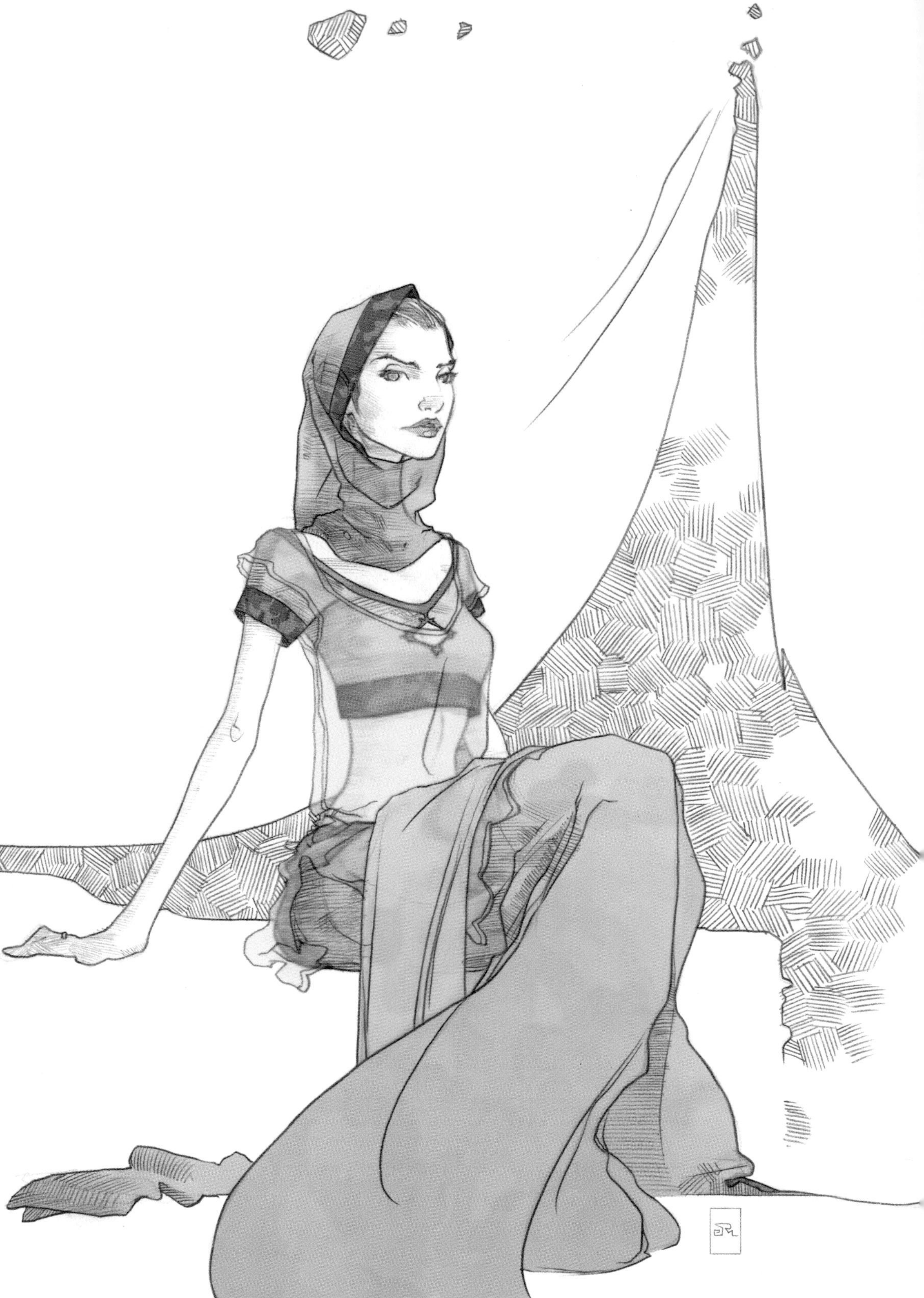

Art by Joshua Middleton

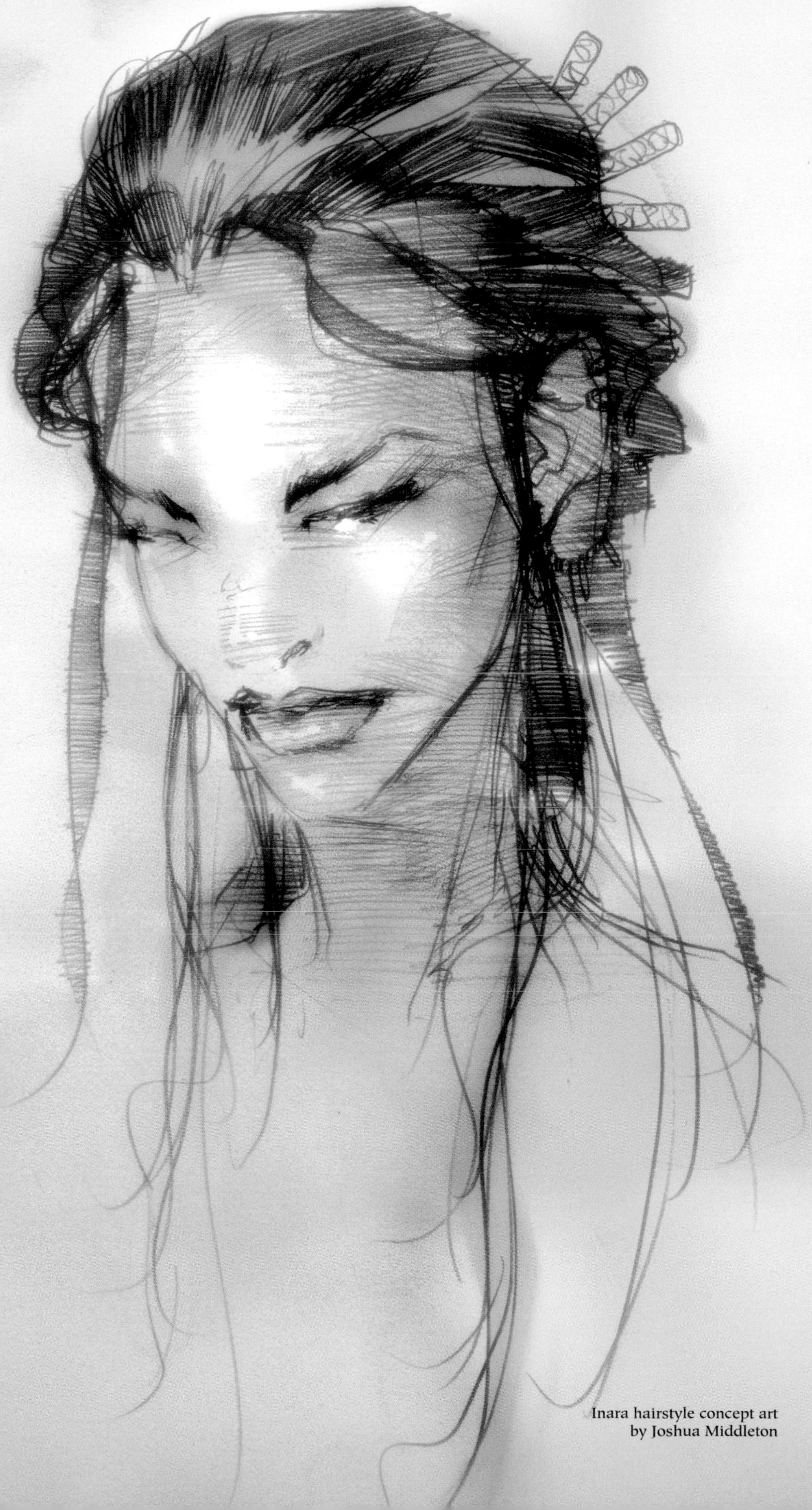

Inara hairstyle concept art
by Joshua Middleton

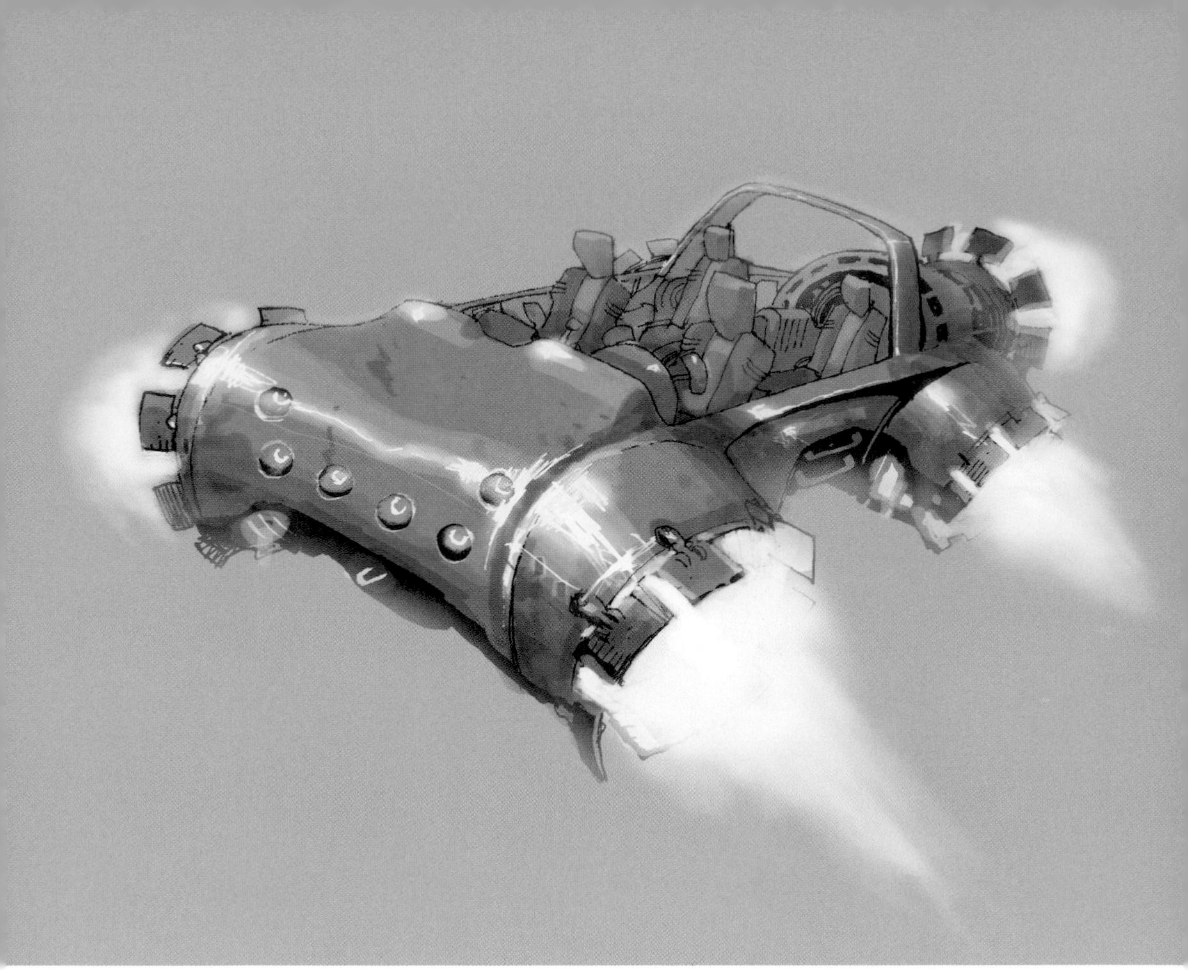

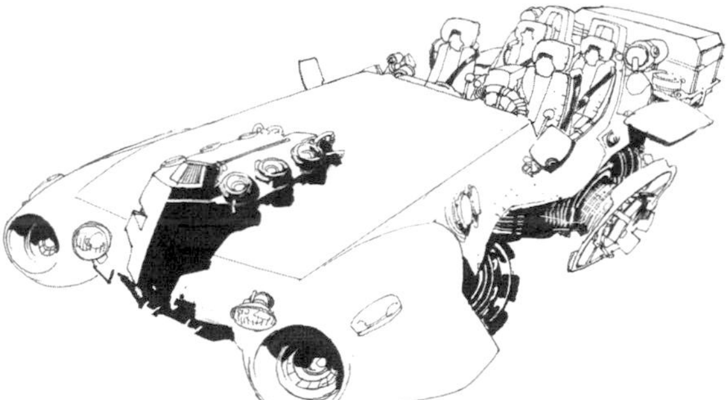

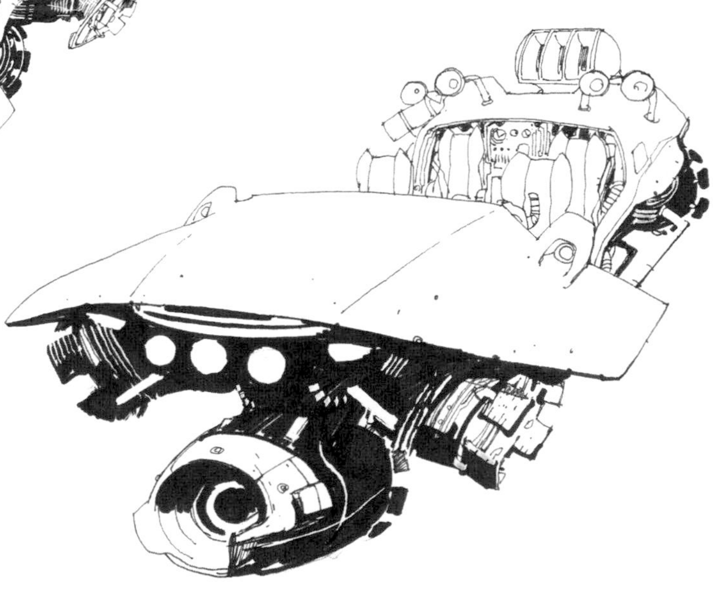

New Mule concept art
by Leinil Francis Yu

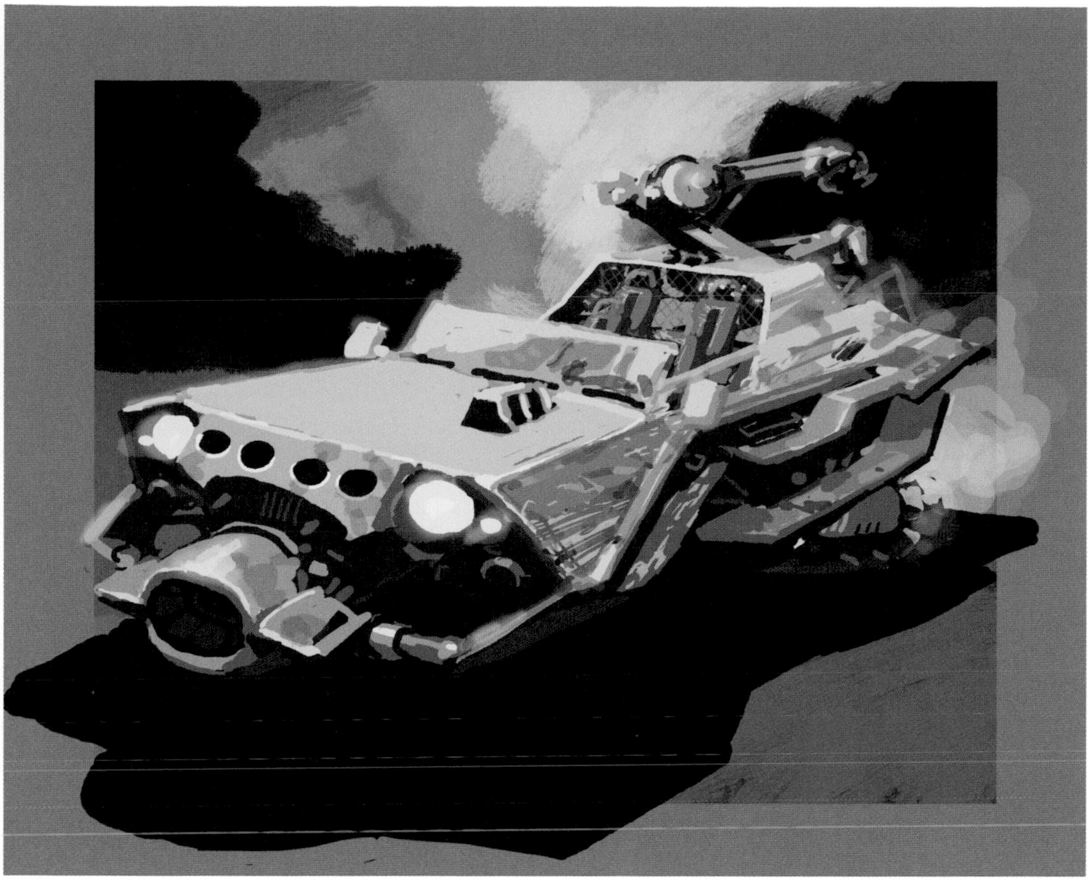

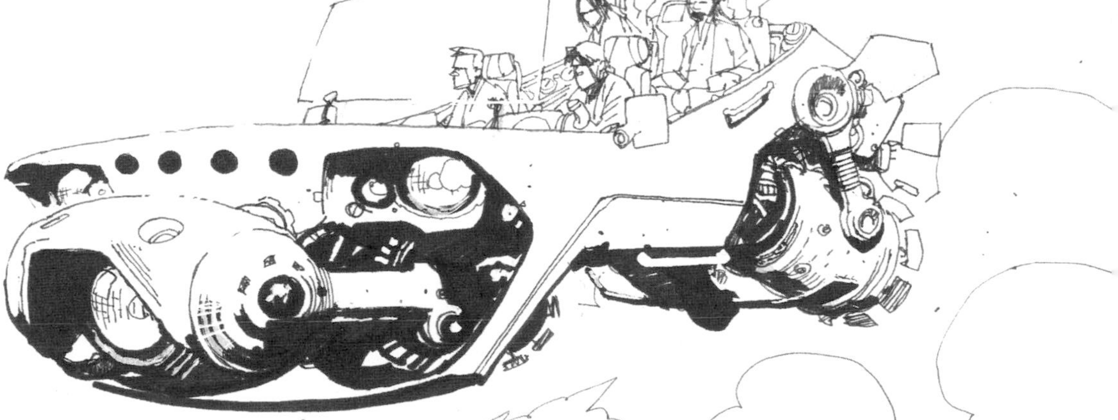

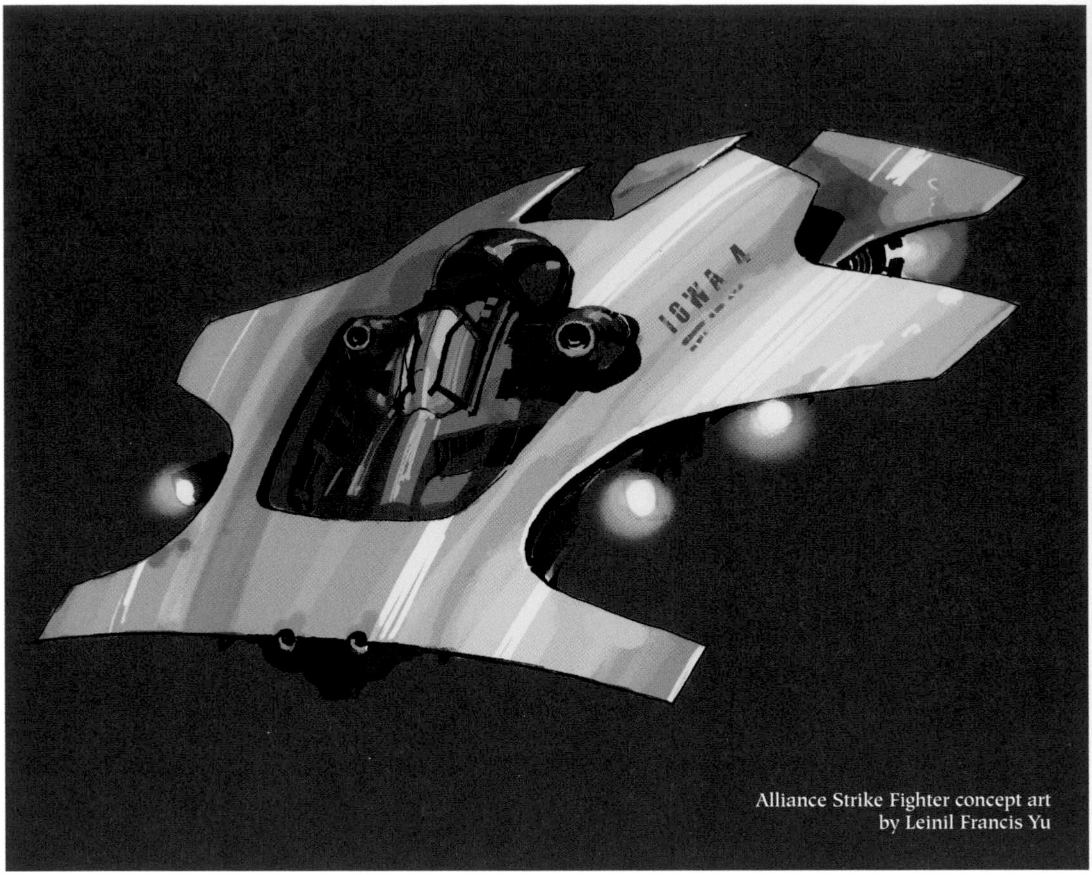
IOWA 4

Alliance Strike Fighter concept art
by Leinil Francis Yu

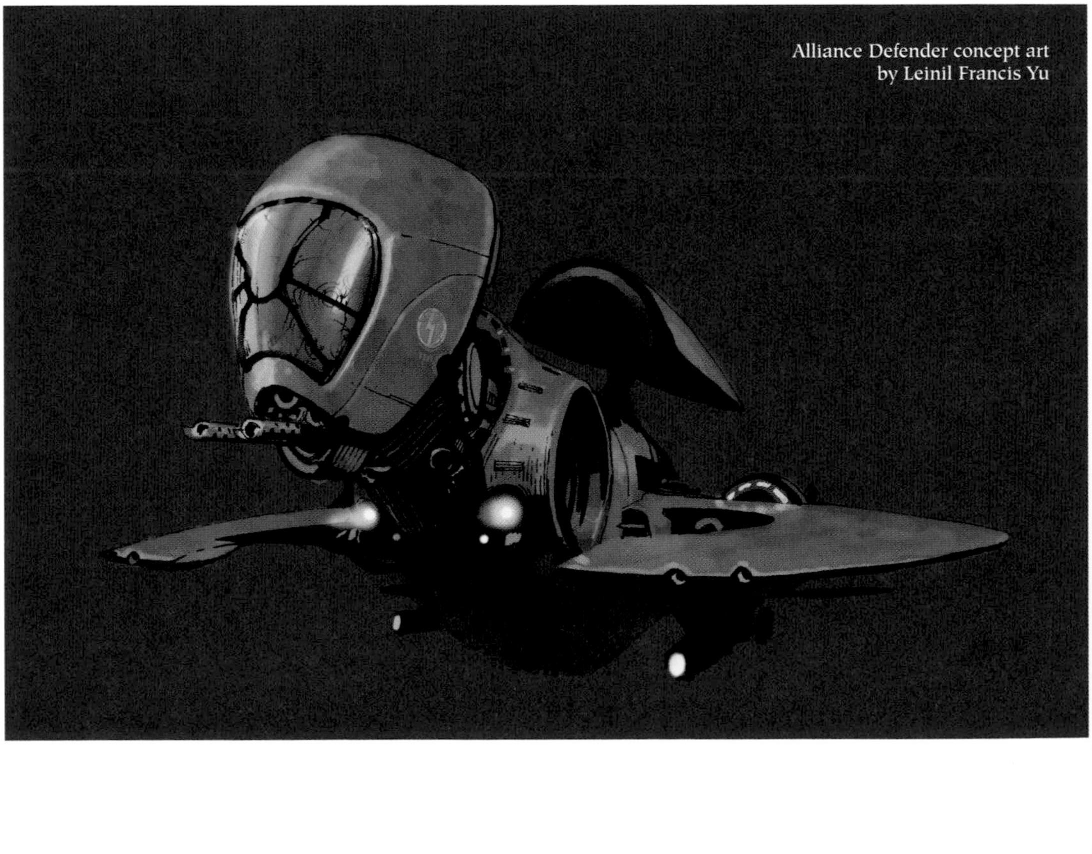

Alliance Defender concept art
by Leinil Francis Yu

Alliance Destroyer concept art
by Leinil Francis Yu

unlike nuns, worked not unlike geishas, and often rose to political or social prominence when
they retired.

Such was life on the central planets: among
them Sihnon, Londinium, and Osiris (where
Simon and River Tam grew up). On the outer
planets, things were a mite different.

The thing is, we had enough worlds to go
around, but not enough resources. And people
didn't exactly stop making babies. The outer
planets, the worlds and moons that hadn't been
chosen to house the new civilization—they were
the destination for the poorer, the more extreme,
the pioneers. They traveled out to the nearest
planet someone hadn't claimed yet and started turning their rockets into roofs. Building off
whatever the land had been shaped to provide
them with. Some of these people were brought
near to savagery by the conditions they encoun-
tered. Some were just hard-working, independent folk who didn't want their lives mapped
out for them before they'd lived them. Didn't

want convenience. Some were orthodox in their
beliefs to the point where they were not comfort-
able among nonbelievers, and wanted worlds
where they would not be slowly homogenized
into the ruling society. And some had reason to
avoid the law.

There were troubles. There were famines; there
were wars—the human race didn't get better
or smarter just 'cause they had made scientific
leaps. Things were definitely more peaceful
amongst the central planets, but that peace was
bought at a price. Nothing resembling totalitari-
anism, but a certain regulation of existence that
would not sit well with some. And even among
these planets, conflicts over resources, trade,
and political influence strained the civil rela-
tions of sister nations. In an effort to unite and
quell this conflict, the central planets formed
the ALLIANCE, a governing structure that uni-
fied them all under one governing body, the
PARLIAMENT. The few members represented
each planet, and worked in genuine harmony to

Science Vessel concept art
by Leinil Francis Yu

fulfill each planet's various needs, economically and politically. In harmony, and very often, in secrecy.

For we are nothing more than human, however high we reach. The Parliament ruled over the people with fairness and intelligence, but also with a strong army and a wary eye toward any insurrection. The MILITARY COUNCIL worked under the Parliament to deliver swift, effective control of any real unrest among them or their neighbors. And even beyond the knowledge of the Military Council were other bodies, secret bodies . . . human experimentation. Spies. Assassins. Schemes, secret up to the highest level, to get people to behave. To improve.

The real trouble started when the Alliance started to look beyond its borders to the worlds around them. Partially out of a desire to see life improved there (and it *was* often unnecessarily barbaric), to bring all the planets into the fold of enlightenment, and partially out of a simple imperialistic wish for control and need for resources offlimits to them, the Parliament—and the Allied planets as a whole—decided that *every* planet should become part of their program. Should be an Alliance planet, whether they wanted to or not.

The War for Unification was the most devastating in human history. Outer planets such as Hera (where the Battle of Serenity was fought), Persephone, and Shadow mustered forces—more than half volunteers—to stop what they felt to be nothing more than imperialist hegemony. For almost five years the war tore into the planets between the central ones and the rim worlds (fighting never reached such pissant moons as Whitefall or Beaumonde, nor did it ever touch Sihnon or Londinium, except in the odd protest or terrorist act). The forces of the Alliance had the technology and the weapons to overcome almost any foe. But they never expected the kind of resistance the other planets could provide. They did not expect so many men and women to still consider freedom worth dying for.

Malcolm Reynolds was on Shadow, living on the cattle ranch his mother ran, when he joined up.

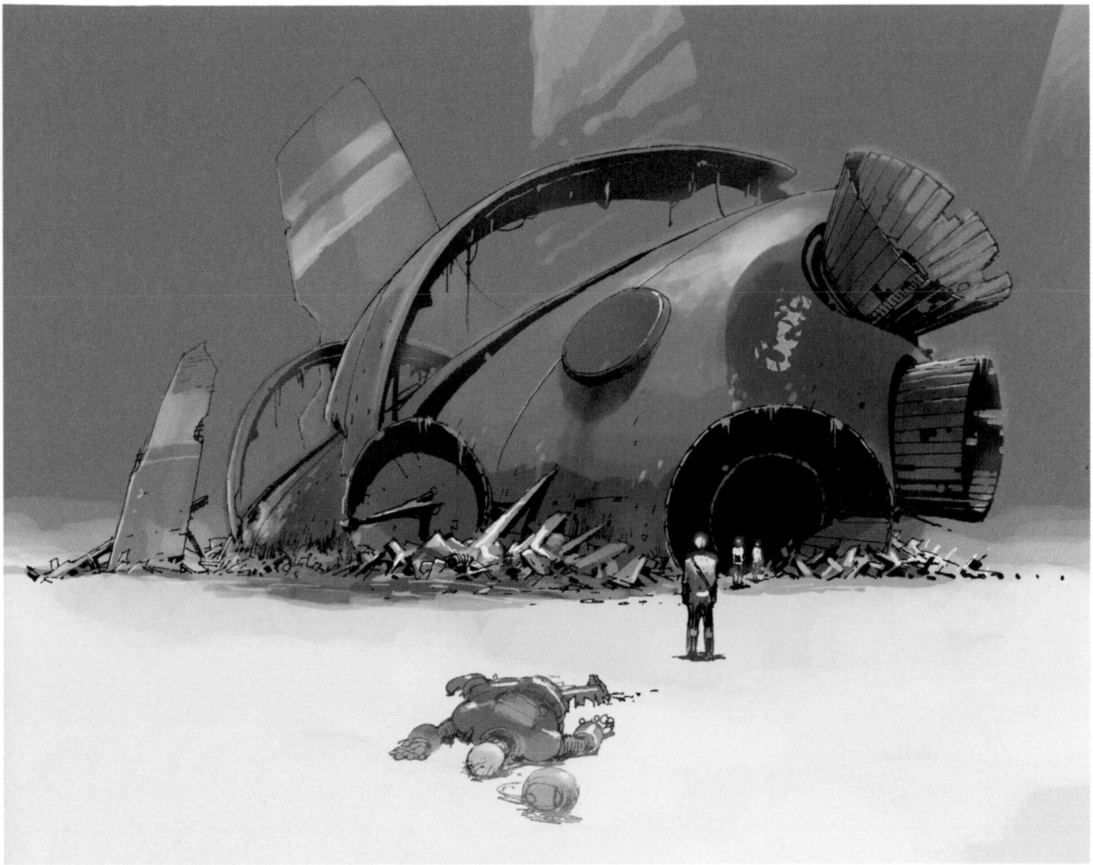

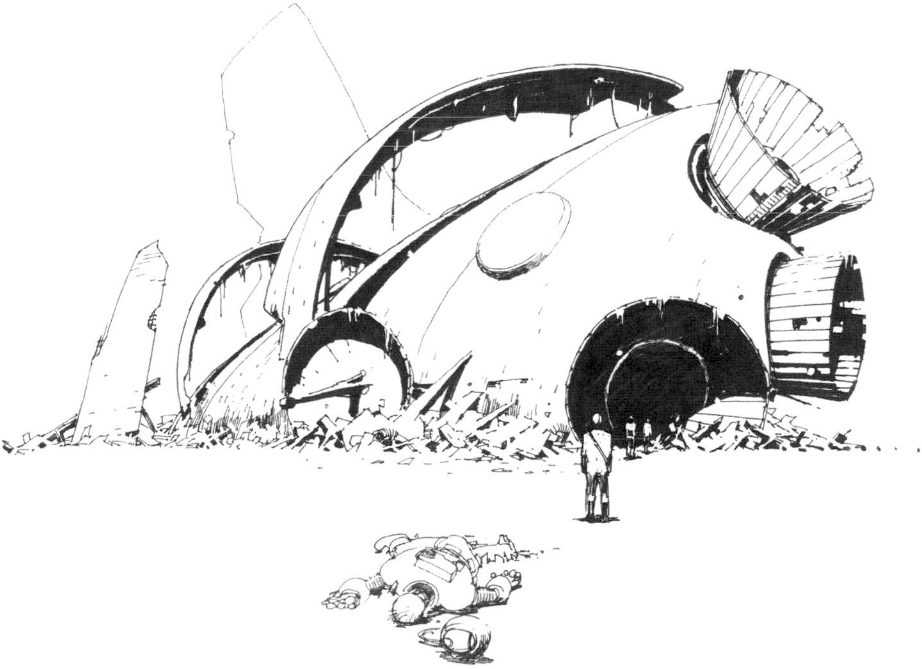

Downed Science Vessel concept
art by Leinil Francis Yu

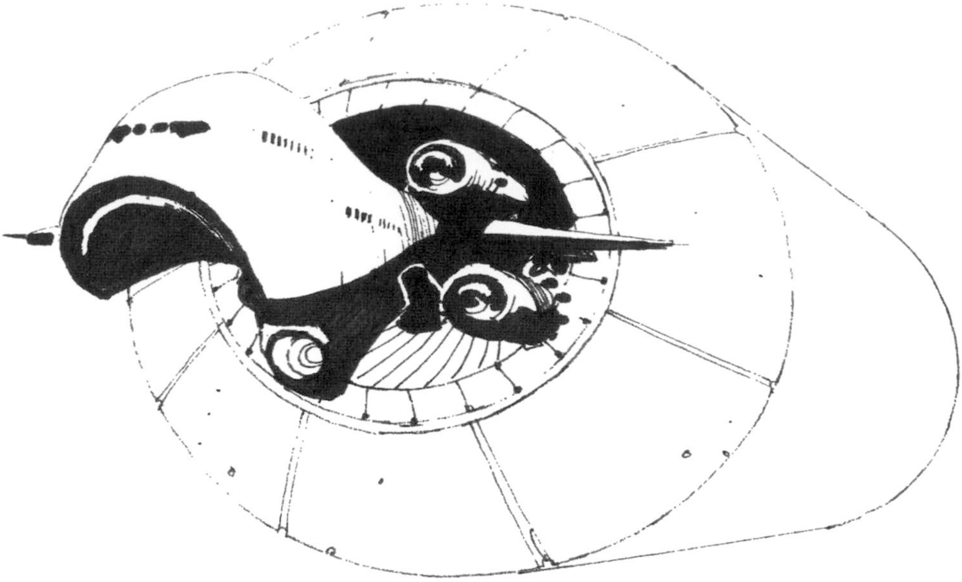

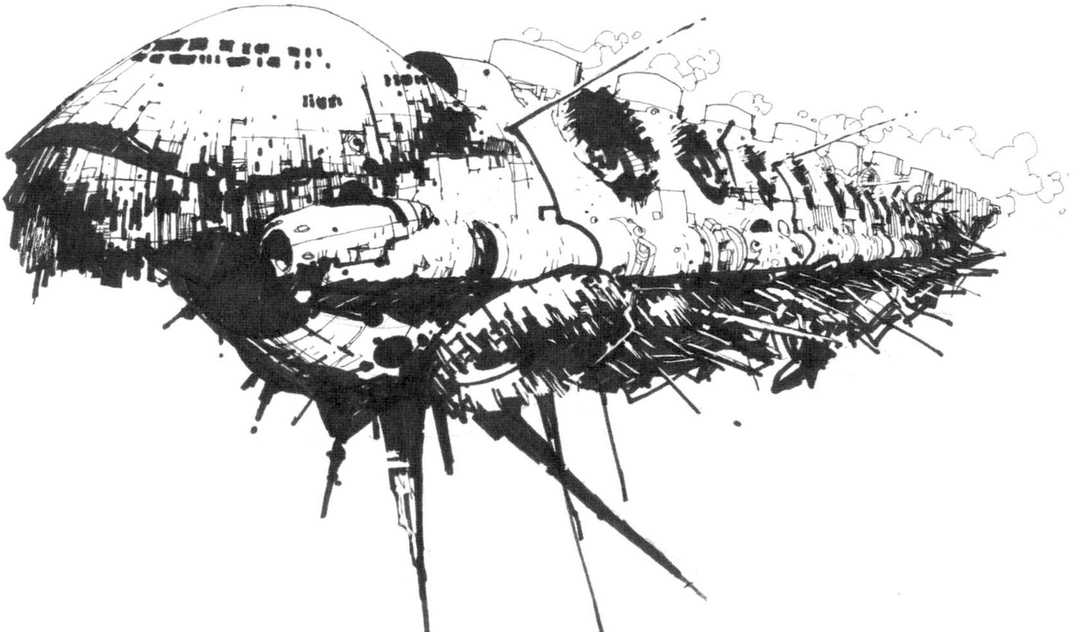

Reaver Destroyer Ship concept art
by Leinil Francis Yu

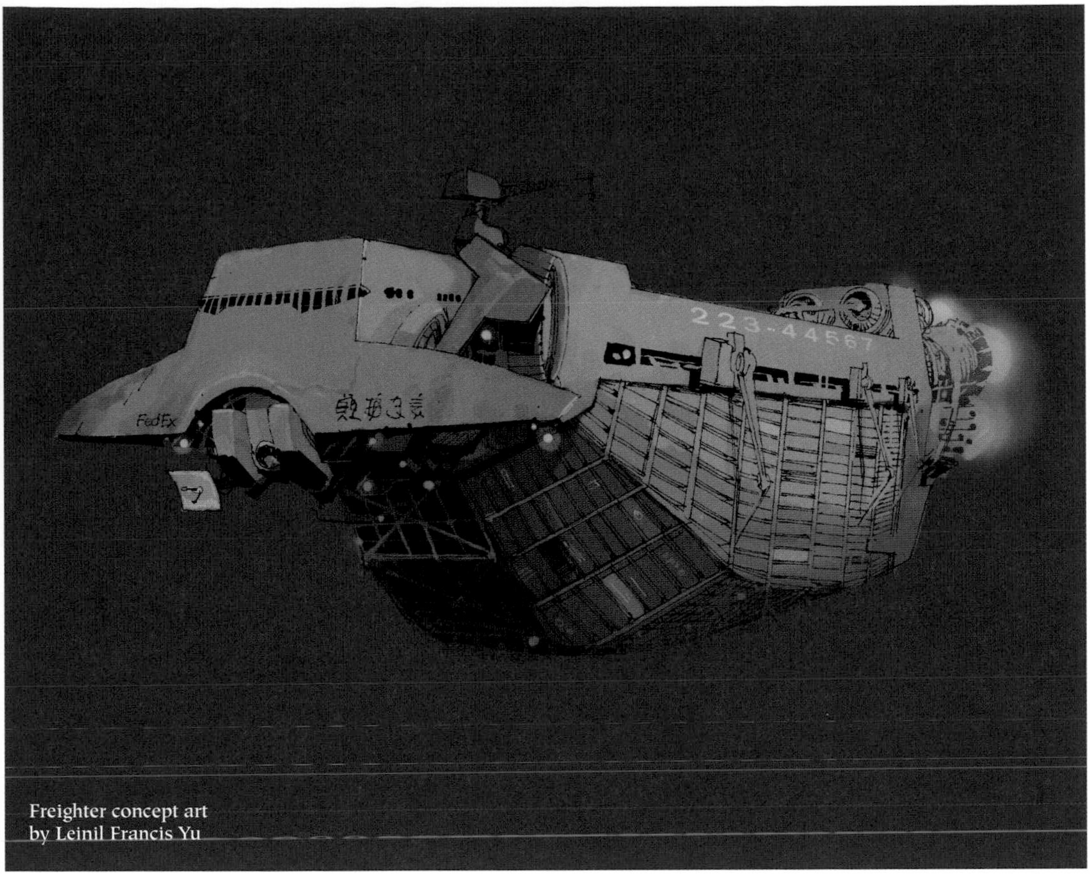
223-44567
FedEx

Freighter concept art
by Leinil Francis Yu

He was a smart kid but green. He joined out of belief and nothing more. Five years gone found his homeworld destroyed, his army beaten down, and every shred of belief ripped out of him. He had made sergeant by then, of the Fifty-seventh Overlanders. Would have gone higher if he had ever kept a single opinion to himself. But he wasn't in the war to get a title. He was there to fight, and in the Battle of Serenity, waged for seven grueling weeks on Hera, he fought like nobody else. Some say that valley was the bridge between the worlds, and that when it fell the Independents fell with it. Surely Mal believed it, for he and his held the valley for a good two weeks *after* the Independent High Command had already surrendered.

When it was all done, there was some talk of branding the "Browncoats" such as Mal who had held Serenity Valley as war criminals, since the war had officially ended. They were held in camps for a short time, but the Alliance considered it an important gesture to free them. The stain of criminality never left those few thousand—but in some quieter circles, the legend of their tenacity made them heroes.

Among those few thousand was Corporal Zoe Alleyne, also of the Fifty-seventh Ovelanders. She had been career army, the opposite of Mal, but she had fought under him for the last two and a half years of the war, in more than a dozen campaigns. She also had the distinction of being the only other member of the Fifty-seventh to survive Serenity. When Mal decided to get himself a little transport ship and head out to the rim worlds, to work the planets the Alliance would not truly be able to control, to settle down never and draw breath free . . . it never occurred to her not to follow him. It also never occurred to her that they would hire a pilot as annoying as Hoban Washburne, or that she would fall so completely in love with him. They were married not a year after they met, an occurrence that Mal considered illadvised and slightly weird.

Wash turned out to be an extraordinary pilot, and they happened (it's a funny story) on a little prodigy of a mechanic, Kaywinnit Lee

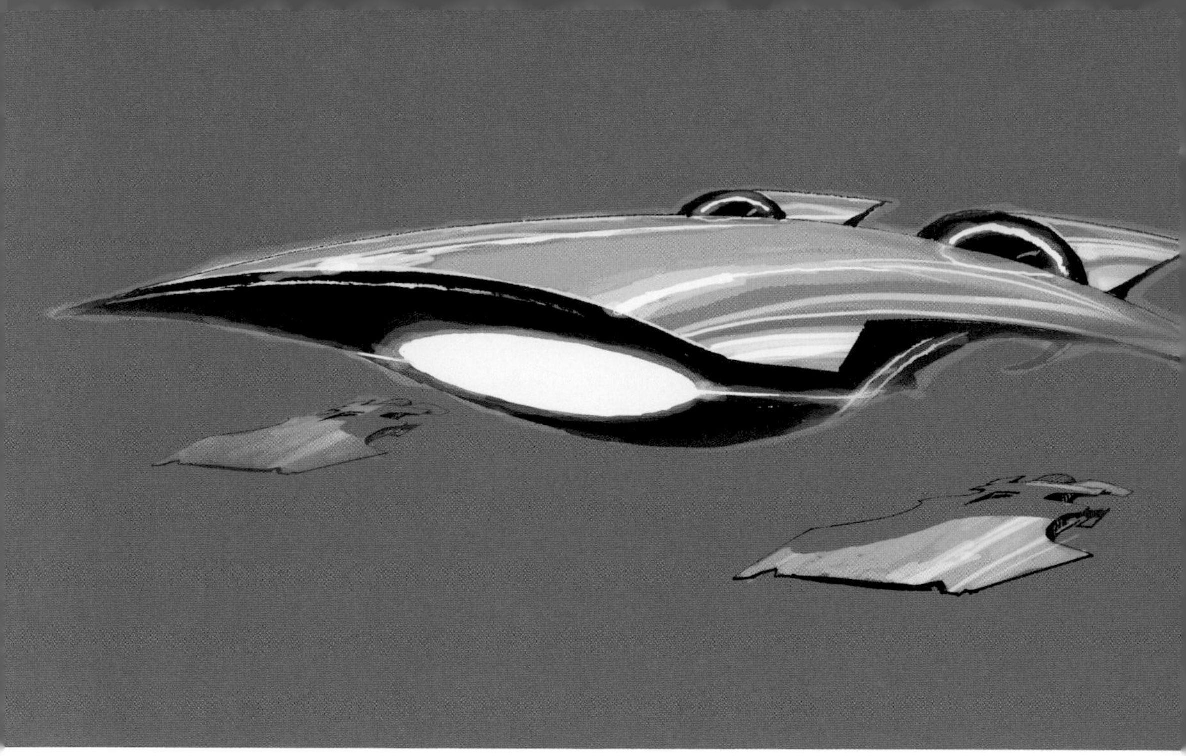

Frye, known as Kaylee. As sweet and cheerful as she was mechanical, she found the opportunity to be chief engineer (a title she used only to herself) on a Firefly-class ship to be beyond her best imaginings. Most folk wouldn't look twice at a Firefly—it had since been replaced by sleeker, more efficient models, but she knew, as Mal did, that a Firefly could hold up where others would buckle . . . that she could get in and out of places other ships couldn't, and quickly too . . . that she was just right for the kind of jobs nobody was supposed to be doing anymore.

'Cause a lot of the work to be found on the border planets was crime, and that was no problem for Mal. He expected it, and he prepared for it. He found himself a great lug of a mercenary in Jayne Cobb: mean, untrustworthy, and indispensable. On the flip side, they actually landed a passenger who could lend them respectability: A first-rate Companion, Inara Serra, who had left House Madrassa on Sihnon to work independently. She never did say why.

Then one day they took on a Shepherd named Book and a young doctor from Osiris named Simon Tam, who had his sister River hidden in a cryogenic box for some damn reason. And that is, of course, another story.

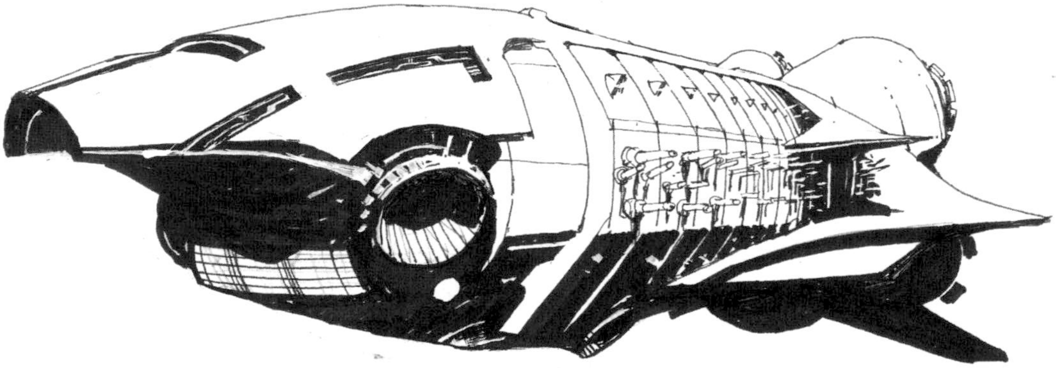

ALSO FROM JOSS WHEDON

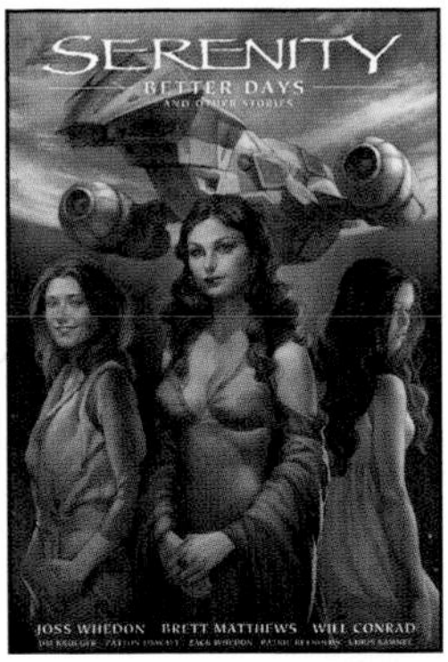
SERENITY
BETTER DAYS
AND OTHER STORIES
JOSS WHEDON BRETT MATTHEWS WILL CONRAD

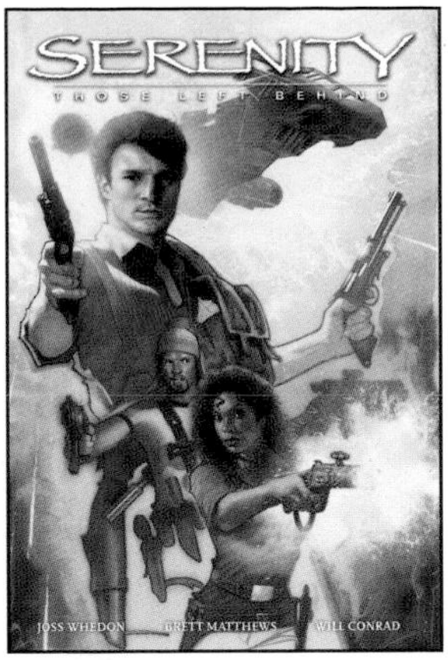
SERENITY
THOSE LEFT BEHIND
JOSS WHEDON BRETT MATTHEWS WILL CONRAD

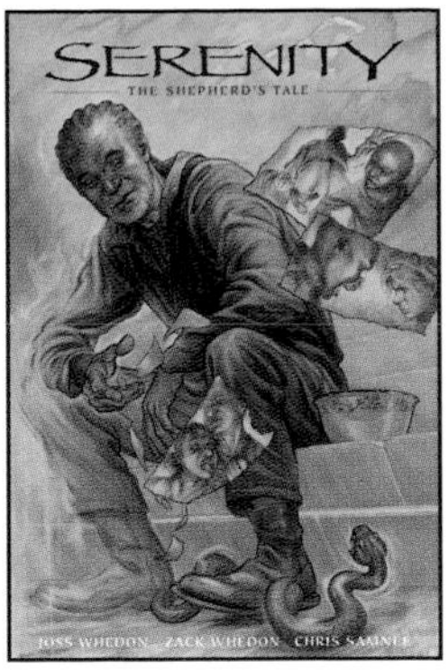
SERENITY
THE SHEPHERD'S TALE
JOSS WHEDON ZACK WHEDON CHRIS SAMNEE

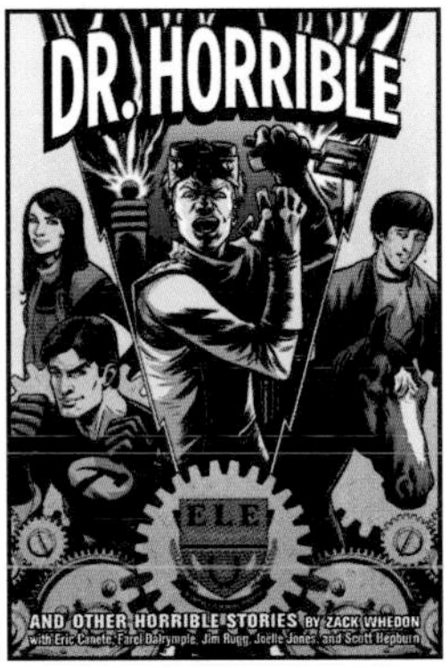
DR. HORRIBLE
E.L.E.
AND OTHER HORRIBLE STORIES BY ZACK WHEDON
with Eric Canete, Farel Dalrymple, Jim Rugg, Joëlle Jones, and Scott Hepburn

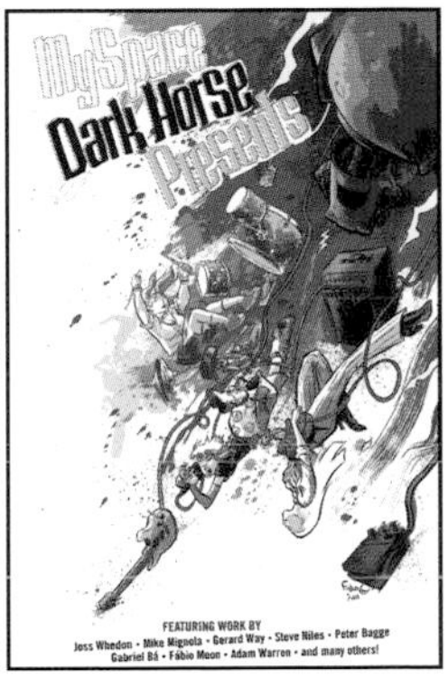
MySpace
Dark Horse
Presents
FEATURING WORK BY
Joss Whedon • Mike Mignola • Gerard Way • Steve Niles • Peter Bagge
Gabriel Bá • Fábio Moon • Adam Warren • and many others!

SERENITY VOLUME 1: THOSE LEFT BEHIND
SECOND EDITION HARDCOVER
Joss Whedon, Brett Matthews, and Will Conrad
ISBN 978-1-59307-846-1 $17.99

SERENITY VOLUME 2: BETTER DAYS AND
OTHER STORIES HARDCOVER
Joss Whedon, Patton Oswalt, Zack Whedon, Patric Reynolds and others
ISBN 978-1-59582-739-5 $19.99

SERENITY VOLUME 3: THE SHEPHERD'S TALE HARDCOVER
Joss Whedon, Zack Whedon, and Chris Samnee
ISBN 978-1-59582-561-2 $14.99

DR. HORRIBLE AND OTHER HORRIBLE STORIES
Joss Whedon, Zack Whedon, Joëlle Jones, and others
ISBN 978-1-59582-577-3 $9.99

MYSPACE DARK HORSE PRESENTS VOLUME 1
Featuring Sugarshock *by Joss Whedon and Fábio Moon*
ISBN 978-1-59307-998-7 $19.99

DOLLHOUSE VOLUME 1: EPITAPHS
Andrew Chambliss, Jed Whedon, Maurissa Tancharoen, and Cliff Richards
ISBN 978-1-59582-863-7 $18.99

DARK HORSE BOOKS
DarkHorse.com

AVAILABLE AT YOUR LOCAL COMICS SHOP OR BOOKSTORE!
TO FIND A COMICS SHOP IN YOUR AREA, CALL 1-888-266-4226.
For more information or to order direct visit DarkHorse.com or call 1-800-862-0052 Mon.–Fri. 9 AM to 5 PM Pacific Time.

FROM JOSS WHEDON

BUFFY THE VAMPIRE SLAYER SEASON 8

VOLUME 1: THE LONG WAY HOME
Joss Whedon and Georges Jeanty
ISBN 978-1-59307-822-5 | $15.99

VOLUME 2: NO FUTURE FOR YOU
Brian K. Vaughan, Georges Jeanty, and Joss Whedon
ISBN 978-1-59307-963-5 | $15.99

VOLUME 3: WOLVES AT THE GATE
Drew Goddard, Georges Jeanty, and Joss Whedon
ISBN 978-1-59582-165-2 | $15.99

VOLUME 4: TIME OF YOUR LIFE
Joss Whedon, Jeph Loeb, Georges Jeanty, and others
ISBN 978-1-59582-310-6 | $15.99

VOLUME 5: PREDATORS AND PREY
Joss Whedon, Jane Espenson, Cliff Richards, Georges Jeanty, and others
ISBN 978-1-59582-342-7 | $15.99

VOLUME 6: RETREAT
Joss Whedon, Jane Espenson, Cliff Richards, Georges Jeanty, and others
ISBN 978-1-59582-415-8 | $15.99

VOLUME 7: TWILIGHT
Joss Whedon, Brad Meltzer, and Georges Jeanty
ISBN 978-1-59582-558-2 | $16.99

VOLUME 8: LAST GLEAMING
Joss Whedon, Scott Allie, and Georges Jeanty
ISBN 978-1-59582-610-7 | $16.99

BUFFY THE VAMPIRE SLAYER SEASON 9

VOLUME 1: FREEFALL
Joss Whedon, Andrew Chambliss, Cliff Richards, Georges Jeanty, and others
ISBN 978-1-59582-922-1 | $17.99

TALES OF THE SLAYERS
Joss Whedon, Amber Benson, Gene Colan, P. Craig Russell, Tim Sale, and others
ISBN 978-1-56971-605-2 | $14.99

TALES OF THE VAMPIRES
Joss Whedon, Brett Matthews, Cameron Stewart, and others
ISBN 978-1-56971-749-3 | $15.99

BUFFY THE VAMPIRE SLAYER: TALES
ISBN 978-1-59582-644-2 | $29.99

FRAY: FUTURE SLAYER
Joss Whedon and Karl Moline
ISBN 978-1-56971-751-6 | $19.99

ALSO FROM DARK HORSE...

BUFFY THE VAMPIRE SLAYER OMNIBUS

VOLUME 1
ISBN 978-1-59307-784-6 | $24.99

VOLUME 2
ISBN 978-1-59307-826-3 | $24.99

VOLUME 3
ISBN 978-1-59307-885-0 | $24.99

VOLUME 4
ISBN 978-1-59307-968-0 | $24.99

VOLUME 5
ISBN 978-1-59582-225-3 | $24.99

VOLUME 6
ISBN 978-1-59582-242-0 | $24.99

VOLUME 7
ISBN 978-1-59582-331-1 | $24.99

ANGEL OMNIBUS
Christopher Golden, Eric Powell, and others
ISBN 978-1-59582-706-7 | $24.99

ANGEL & FAITH VOLUME 1: LIVE THROUGH THIS
Christos Gage, Rebekah Isaacs, Phil Noto, and others
ISBN 978-1-59582-887-3 | $17.99

BUFFY THE VAMPIRE SLAYER: PANEL TO PANEL
ISBN 978-1-59307-836-2 | $19.99

 DARK HORSE BOOKS ®
DarkHorse.com

AVAILABLE AT YOUR LOCAL COMICS SHOP OR BOOKSTOR
To find a comics shop in your area, call 1-888-266-4226.
For more information or to order direct: • On the web: DarkHorse.com • E-m
mailorder@darkhorse.com • Phone: 1-800-862-0052
Mon.–Fri. 9 AM to 5 PM Pacific Time.
*Prices and availability subject to change without notice

Buffy the Vampire Slayer™ & © 1998, 2012 Twentieth Century Fox Film Corporation. All rights reserved. Fray™ & © 2012 Joss Whedon. All rights reserved. (BL 5051)